ROBEI



# I Don't Do That Anymore

*A Memoir of Awakening and Resilience*

# CREDITS

Every effort has been made to contact copyright holders for permission to reproduce borrowed materials where necessary. We apologize for any oversights and would be happy to rectify them in future printings. The names of some persons in this memoir have been changed.

Artwork by Michael Buckley



Printed by CreateSpace
Charleston, South Carolina
Printed in the United States of America

ISBN: 1-4609-5255-3
ISBN-13: 978-1-4609-5255-9
LCCN:

# DEDICATION

For my astounding wife, Sue, who has valiantly borne my ups and downs and has taught me all I know about family.

And to Marabel Beck, who redirected my life as a youngster and kept tabs on me and supported me the rest of her life.

And to Charles King Hart, who loved me enough to reengage with me after letting me go as a foster child then becoming my legal father when I was 60.

*In loving memory of*

## Charles King Hart

1909 — 2002

# TABLE OF CONTENTS

# PREFACE

Lacking knowledge of family history, I have worried a lot throughout my life about various possible health issues, such as cancer, heart disease, Alzheimer's or madness. Particularly madness, for once when I was a boy in a children's home I banged my head against the shower wall and was told by a kid taking freshman psychology that I was crazy and named several likely illnesses I might have. I worried that I was a sissy or a homo (a 12-year-old had pushed me into a closet and attempted a rape and when I was 15 a dance instructor got me drunk and tried to take advantage of me) or that I was nasty (my mother's word when she caught me doing preschool body exploration as a frail little boy). I worried that I wouldn't live up to expectations (mostly my own).

I worried that people wouldn't like me, and, in fact, when I was a young man I believed that whenever someone spent enough time in my company that person would begin to dislike me. I worried that, at the core, I was undeserving and not a good person—something I learned later that I shared with a lot of children ( now adults) whose parents had divorced, or who had lost a sibling, were molested, have attention deficit disorder or have endured other experiences that put them at a higher risk of unfulfilled lives than the general population. I worried that I was going to kill my mother when she made comments such as "Couldn't they have given you a bigger desk?" when she visited my first classroom when I was an elementary school teacher, an achievement that made me so proud but, from her first reaction, I interpreted as my not being good enough.

But the topic of mother I will save for later. By the time I was 2, this woman, Eleanore, was the third of four mothers I was to have. I blamed a lot of my failings, shortcomings, and the way I was on this "tragic" childhood until I was nearly 40. At 40 I discovered the word "responsibility" applied to me.

This is a story of my life. From the perspective of 77 years now, it feels like a gift. I write it to understand why I am here—healthy; reasonably well-adjusted and successful—when so many of my childhood friends are not. I write it to learn more about my own story and who I am among all the roles I've played, postures I've assumed, masks I've adopted. I write it to cease having the stories from my past become a limitation to my further development. I write it in preparation for the end of life. I also write it because my family has encouraged me for years to do so.

I am neither unbiased in recounting my story nor an expert in the study of human development. Nor do I have an infallible memory. In fact, there are huge gaps in what I recall, in part because of my former drug and alcohol use and in part because of a seeming predilection I have to forget events large and small. A therapist once told me that I have "cauterized" many childhood feelings. Perhaps some will open as I write this.

Friends tell me that the story of my childhood and my fits and starts of adult growth make an interesting tale. I hope this is true. I also hope if someone reading this might know a youth who is behaving as I did or a young adult making mistakes like mine that perhaps this story will remind them of the inevitability of human resilience—that given even the slightest help, most young people challenged with life turn out all right.

Most children, even those from an extraordinarily stressed family or resource-deprived community, somehow manage to make decent lives for themselves. According to experts, as many as seven out of ten kids from populations at greater risk than others have managed to achieve decent lives by the time they are 40. Even adolescents who had developed serious coping problems, as I had done with alcohol, have managed to overcome them by mid-life.

I was fortunate to have several adults take an interest in me. At 15, I was placed with a foster family. I was so difficult that my foster parents were forced to have me leave. But they didn't give up on me. Nor did my social worker, who kept an eye on my life and intervened at several critical moments even after I was old enough to vote. Had these adults despaired of me because of my mistakes, these events would have been life altering and my story would be dramatically different.

The sense of "badness" I felt came from my behaviors at that time and the emotional abuse that had thus far shaped me. My adoptive home had been a place of tension and fighting. I was considered enough of a problem to be placed in a special education class at age 7 and then, over the course of the next two years, be admitted and later expelled from a group home in

Glendale, California. After that I was shuffled off to live with an aunt in Oakland, California.

In total, I spent nine years of my young life away from home. Three of these began at age seven. Five years were spent at Lytton Home, then one year with a foster family. Lytton was an institution for troubled boys and girls run by the Salvation Army in California. It is no longer in existence. It was not a bad place but a place where I had some bad experiences. There were certainly things wrong at Lytton—unqualified staff, which is why it was shut down years later, two pedophiles we kids knew about, and beatings—and yet there were positive things that I remember making an impact on me as well. The best of these were summer camping and roaming the creeks and hills behind the facility, which were forested with oak, bay and Manzanita trees.

My attitudes toward authority at the home were nothing less than combative. Others at Lytton, my first wife's sister, for example, say that it was a pleasant port in a storm. Earlier, she and Irene, my first wife had been in a foster home, where they were treated as servants for a couple who gave them bed and board but did not show any interest in them nor gave them any affection. It was also a better place to be than in Juvenile Detention, where some kids came from before Lytton.

While writing this memoir, I met a man who was housed at Lytton five years earlier than I was. His father was Japanese. He recalled that one day the FBI arrived at his home in San Francisco and took him and his brother away, without telling their mother where they were being taken. He said she fretted so much about their unknown whereabouts and finally was able to convince the authorities that her 9- and 7-year-old sons were too young to be spies. Instead of being sent to a Japanese reclamation camp, as planned they were sent to Lytton. He describes his time there as nearly idyllic. In spite of being thrown against the wall by one of the deans and slapped around occasionally, he still found this a better place to be than where he was before.

One didn't have to grow up in a children's home to experience some sense of distress. Most of the people we meet have a story behind the faces they present to others. My wife Sue's mother committed suicide, leaving an ache in Sue's heart about the absence of a mother and grandmother for her children. King

Hart, my second adoptive father, bemoaned the fact that he never completed college, and it bothered him until the end of his life. In my work as a teacher, school principal, university professor, author and educational consultant I am astounded when I learn of the difficulties people cope with, the troubles that are generally never revealed for public consumption.

Recently, a person I knew from the Navy wrote to me unexpectedly. I had not seen or heard of him for 55 years, and yet he said,

> *"I really haven't as yet found, and will most probably not find, the words to tell you how very, very proud I am of you, and very happy for you.*
>
> *I might even say that I have thought of you on many occasions through the years; and, I have been proud of your accomplishments for at least the last twenty-five years.*
>
> *Your achievements are much greater than I could have ever have seen or understood."*

His note shocked me. How did he know what I had been doing for the past half century? Of course, he could not have predicted my achievements, because any snapshot of a life cannot possibly tell a full story or look into the future—especially one taken of a rootless kid between the ages of 17 and 20 who had no goals, no prospects and a chip on his shoulder as large as the Navy itself.

# CHAPTER 1

## *Who Was I?*

The stolen birth certificate felt like contraband marijuana inside my pocket. Footsteps echoed on the polished floor in the cavernous public room. People were hushed as they went about their business while I, with taps on my shoes, clattered my way across the lobby and out the front door. Tucked in my coat pocket was the birth certificate I had taken from the file when the clerk stepped away from the desk. I walked out of the courthouse into the San Diego sunshine with the same paranoid feelings I had when smoking dope. I told myself to walk slowly, normally, as if nothing was wrong. At the corner, I turned and moved toward the water, the sounds of the harbor close by.

I was 15, wearing slacks and a sports coat, trying to look older. I was astonished that the clerk responded to my request for the file and even more surprised when he stepped away to let me browse it in private. Maybe it was the deep voice I affected.

Outside, I scanned its contents. There were more than just adoption papers. One section was about John and Eleanore Garmston, who were filing for adoption. Another woman was mentioned—Merle May Day, John's first wife, who died when "baby boy Brown," as I was called, was 7 months old. The name of the hospital and other official stuff I didn't take the time to look at because I had only one thing in mind: find my birth parents. Finally, there it was—a certificate of birth for Robert John Garmston, born November 24, 1933, in San Diego County, California.

Several blocks later, I stopped to read more, still amazed to have it in my possession. Anyone seeing me would not have taken much notice. I was slim and of moderate height, with dirty blond hair that was slicked back into a duck's ass. I wore shiny black shoes built up with enough tacks on the soles and the heels that I could slide-skate in school hallways, which is what I did until I dropped out in the fall of my junior year, and, like my friends, I spit shined and buffed them until they gleamed like glass.

I remember standing on that littered street, with the smells of the fishing boats at the wharf drifting in on the breeze. The only thing on my mind was to learn about my birth parents and track them down. What would I do then? Try to see them? Ask them questions? Why did they give me away?

With trepidation I read further. Mother's name—Gladys Smith. Father's name—Fredrick Brown. Shit! Smith and Brown—clearly made-up names so the shame of what they'd done could not be traced. Their ages at the time of my birth were 38 and 49, respectively. Father, a retired oil worker from Ohio. I read further and some hope sparked. The doctor's name was Thomas S. Whitlock, Jr. and an address in San Diego was given. I could find him.

Mickey Spillane was my favorite mystery writer, and so I thought I had learned enough about sleuthing from his novels to follow the clue of the doctor's name to learn more about my parents. This first leg of my investigation led to crushing disappointment. Dr. Whitlock was dead. I looked at my birth certificate again and noticed something I had missed before. It read, "Was a prophylactic used?" Written on the answer line was the word "Yes." If so, it asked, "What kind?" "Silver nitrate." It seems funny now, but upon first seeing those words on my birth certificate I believed that not only was I born out of wedlock, a euphemism for being a bastard, but I had been strained through a rubber as well! It was much, much later that I learned that silver nitrate was sometimes used on a baby's eyes to prevent infection.

# CHAPTER 2

## *Mother Number Three*

*John and Bobby Garmston*

## ELEANORE

*Old thin arms*
*on hospital sheets*
*I wish no reawakening*
*to seductive hopes of your love*

*You are a flower wilted.*
*You shared with me in your bloom*
*the tearing, painful thorns of dreams undreamt*
*Clenched petals constricted*
*your intelligent face*
*fragile shelter from cruel storms*
*visited upon you in your childhood.*

*Inside you wished to dance*
*emerald light in open fields*
*flower fragrances*
*and tried to share these*
*but they were trapped, distorted in your*
*own pained  and lonely journey*

*Eyes dry and distant*
*no channel open to free my tears*
*forgive my detached calm, mother*
*my polite caring*
*at your bedside*

*—RJG*

Forgiveness means you have no need to hurt or punish. For years, I punished Eleanore—in my mind, in talking about her, and in drunken phone calls to her late at night.

Eleanore was the third of four mothers I was destined to have. Mother number two died in my seventh month. It must have been initially difficult for my father, grieving the death of his young wife and coping with infant care while performing his duties as a Radioman in the Navy. The arrangements for my placement with John and Merle May Garmston occurred in November when I was 4 days old and the adoption occurred almost four months later on March 14. By July Merle May appears on John's Navy records as deceased. I assume infant care was complicated for John after her death. His Navy records show requests to transport his infant son, his dependent mother and 17-year-old sister on the U.S.S. Henderson from New Haven, Connecticut to San Francisco. His sister Alice was present because his mother, Ida Mae Garmston was ill and not able to care for me on the voyage. I don't know when John and Eleanore married though court records show that she adopted me and is listed as John's dependent in August of 1935. I was one year and five months of age.

I know little about John Garmston. He graduated from eighth grade, and lied about his age to enlist in the Navy. As a young man he seized opportunities for training in radio, and continued this pattern throughout his career. His service record is replete with permissions to attend a variety of courses. Sometimes these were off base with per diems granted ($1.00 per day). John eventually was promoted through the ranks to Lt. Commander, the rank he held when he died of a heart attack in 1952. He was on active service throughout my childhood years and served, as is typical of armed forces personnel, on a variety of stations and ships. While reviewing family documents I learned he had a brother and a sister. I have no knowledge of their lives. His family came from Connecticut.

Eleanore said she took pity on this little boy who needed a haircut and a mother, and so she married John when I was 17 months old. I lived with her continuously until age 7, when sister Lynne was born. Then I began a series of placements outside our home—to special education classes, group homes, one year living with an aunt and finally a half year with a foster family.

As a young adult I punished Eleanore for abandoning me, for rejection, for letting me know that I was not good enough, no matter what I had accomplished. I punished her for her frailties and played on her paranoia, saying in a conspiratorial telephone voice, "We need to be careful, Mom, *that element* might be listening." *That element* was a reference to the Roman Catholic Church, which she was certain had gone through her personnel files to insert false negative reports and remove positive ones when she was working.

I was critical of her cockeyed prejudicial comments. "Notice how schools are recruiting more teachers from Latin America. More influence for the church." Once she showed me a news clipping she had saved. The photo showed a crashed automobile with a St. Christopher medal hanging from what was left of the rear-view mirror. "More lies," she said, "to enslave the people. No safety from that medal. None at all." Unconsciously, she practiced a kind of reverse racism. Walking to church in the morning, she would grip my 7-year-old arm and whisper, "Look at that colored person over there. He is just as good as you and me."

I punished my mother because she embarrassed me. I punished her because as a child I wanted to be home and not away at some institution. I tried to cause her pain because I hurt so much, had cried my way through countless therapy sessions and encounter groups in my 20s and early 30s, and I punished her because I blamed her for all the miserableness of my life.

## ELEANORE'S BACKGROUND

Eleanore Lillian Olson came to the San Francisco Bay area with her sister Violet when they were in their early 20s. From a farm family in Idaho, Eleanore was the fifth of eight children. They were all schooled in the beliefs of Christian Science and clung to proof of the power of mind over body. Both girls were bright, attractive, and courageous. Violet soon got a job with the telephone company, where she worked until she retired, and she died sometime in her 60s. I think Eleanore worked there as well. My sister Lynne, who was born when I was 7, wrote to me that Eleanore also worked at Western Union at the St. Francis Hotel in Union Square, and she believes it was probably the only happy time in Eleanore's life. Both Eleanore and Violet were slim but not slight and quite tall, about 5'8 or so. From a photograph of Eleanore as a young lady she appears to be strikingly beautiful.

Eleanore's parents were of Scandinavian stock. Her father left Denmark to escape the draft into the country's mercenary army, possibly in the 1890s. Eleanore's mother, Alice Ann Christopherson, was part Swedish and part Danish. She met her husband to be in Minnesota, and they homesteaded in Moody Creek, Montana. After they ran into money problems, they moved to St. Anthony, Idaho where Walter, their youngest child, was born. The other siblings in addition to Violet and Eleanore, were Irving, Harvey, Raymond, Sarah, Babs, and Walter.

It was ironic that her father, said to be immensely strong, died from a simple hernia operation. This reinforced the anxiety they felt regarding medical treatment and made prayer an even more important choice. With renewed fervor they attended the Christian Scientist church.

My sister Lynne knows more about Eleanore's siblings than do I. Talking about Ray, she said, "He was homeless for quite a while until Violet took him in at her little house in Oakland. He lived there till Violet died, and then Eleanore made arrangements for him to go to a home, where he died. To her credit, Eleanore did everything she could to care for both Violet and later Ray, and she didn't complain about it much. But it was hard for her. I think Ray was an autistic savant; he was able to read masses of books and newspapers, remember what he read and where he found it. But Ray was unable to care for himself, or keep a job. He spent a lot of his time riding the buses in Oakland all over the place and in the library. He had a sweet personality. Another sibling was Sarah, who lived in Seattle all her life, married, never had kids, and seemed like a studious and sweet decent sort. Babs lived in Portland most of her life." Lynne thinks several family members had emotional and mental challenges, including Ray, Eleanore and their father.

Eleanore was highly articulate. She loved movies and was fond of chocolate in her later years. But she was more than hard to get along with, especially for me. I don't know if she had been burdened by something in her childhood or just found it difficult to cope with life. As an adolescent, she bound her breasts so they would not grow. Lynne thinks that binding of breasts was common and fashionable in those days. That could be, but given Eleanore's preoccupation with the body and things sexual in her admonishments to me, I think there was more to it. Lynne told me that during the San Francisco period Eleanore had a lovely relationship and became pregnant. She had an abortion. This was so unthinkable in the 1930s that she must have been overwhelmed with shame.

## IN HER EYES, I WAS ALWAYS BAD

*Bobby Garmston, age 7*

"Don't you ever let me see you touching those boys again!" she screamed at me, veins bulging blue in her neck. Looking out of her window on Marlborough Street in San Diego, Eleanore had seen three of us, arms over each other's shoulders, walking home from school. We were in the third grade–the "gang age," some educators call it, when peer relationships begin to take on special importance. This was about the same time that I came home with a new word, "bitchin'," which meant really nice. What I had learned in school that day got me a mouthful of soap that night, cleaning out the dirty words I had dared to bring into the house.

When I was even younger, she had accused me of sitting before her lady friends—they on the couch, me on the floor—so I could look up their dresses. The thought would never have entered my head! What would be of interest under their dresses? Still, I burned with shame and, more than that, with the injustice of being wrongly judged. Her abhorrence of those things physical, and especially sexual, was transmitted to me with unwavering certainty over and over again. In the garage one afternoon, another boy my age and I wanted to know what an asshole looked like. We dropped out pants and had a look. My mother exploded. It was not that the act was wrong—I was! Wrong, dirty, "nasty" (her favorite word), and there had never been anyone as filthy, low and deserving no respect or love than I was. She never caught on that another boy and I played under a nearby house where a little girl let us look up her dress. Or maybe she would have felt better that I was looking at a girl, rather than a boy, but I doubt it. Future events would bear me out.

Once while on a city bus in Seattle when the family lived in that city, Eleanore accused me of shifting in my seat bus so I could stare at that "prostitute." What *was* going on for her? Another time when she told me a lawyer was trying to force a divorce between John and her, she berated me soundly for not crying. Not crying was tantamount, I guess, to not caring. I remember my sister Lynne clinging to Eleanore while I, a skinny teenager, stood frozen in the doorframe of Eleanore's bedroom. What I remember most, however, is not being able to feel anything, other than emptiness, and it scared me.

She pointed out to me frequently that I was selfish. I remember that when I was about 8, father John Garmston was shipped off to sea. World War II had begun only months earlier, and tension was in the air, particularly since we lived in a Navy town. By then San Diego had all its airplane factories placed under camouflage nets lining U.S. 101, the north-south highway.

About this time I recall an experience when John and Eleanore were hugging—a standing-up, tight, concentrated embrace, as if to say will we see each other again? I wiggled into the center of the hug. At the same time a balloon popped, one of mine of course, and I wailed with sorrow over the loss of this wonderful toy. After John left the house on his way to the Navy base, Eleanor berated me for my selfish, self-centered preoccupation with myself. I was not to forget my insensitivity to my father's leaving. For months, I was reminded over and over again how selfish I was. How could I care more about the balloon than the fact that my father—who, I was sure it was said, loved me—was departing? It was not the first time I was made to feel ashamed of myself, nor the last.

Eleanore became the main influence in my life both negative and positive. John was gone to war, and I suspect that he was more comfortable with Navy personnel than he was with his unpredictably emotional wife. My sister Lynne reaffirmed this recently when she told me of their frequent screaming, swearing fights in later years after I was gone.

In my early years with Eleanore, before Lynne was born, She taught me to read. I would sit on her lap; she would read the comic strips with her finger pointing at each word as she read. If I looked away, she would stop reading. As a result, before I was in kindergarten I could read the San Diego Tribune—that is, I could say most of the words even though I didn't really know what I was reading. In my mid-30s, while under hypnosis I was asked to recover an image from childhood. There, in my mind's eye, was a giant finger, tracing underneath a set of words. That was Eleanore.

I may also have received from Eleanore a sense of entrepreneurship. When I was a little boy, she paid me a penny for every two sow bugs that I picked from the victory garden. She encouraged me to set up a lemonade stand in front of our house and would sell me the lemons and sugar to make the drinks. I dragged a red wagon around the neighborhood selling used magazines, and I remember the balls of aluminum foil we traded at the grocery store for cash. I think she had fantasies of my becoming a businessman. She would call me "RJ" (Robert John), because she thought business magnates used initials. When I was 13 and in the eighth grade, one of my friends, Gabby Moore, tattooed those initials on the shin of my right leg late at night in a cottage bathroom, using India ink and a pin.

I ran lawn mowers in the neighborhood before I was old enough to push one. And I felt rich without boundaries, because with my earnings I could see the movie "Snow White and the Seven Dwarfs" seven days in a row, each time hiding when the wicked witch appeared in the mirror on the wall. On movie days I rode a bus out to El Cajon Boulevard to see the films all by myself. I was 8.

Not all of my entrepreneurial efforts were good. One Saturday I raided Eleanore's purse. Feeling incredibly wealthy and important with five dollars of free money I distributed coins and candy to the kids hanging around the movie theater on University

Avenue a couple of blocks from our house. I paid dearly for that afterward, when she discovered the money had disappeared.

I remember, too, that Eleanore took me several times to the San Diego Zoo. These were magical experiences. Past the lions and the tigers, past the monkey cages and popcorn stands, we moved down, down, down into a canyon bordered by tropical plants. Our path ran alongside an enormous screened area that descended along with us. This was a huge aviary, home to birds large and small, bright and brighter, gray and clawed, swooping through the air or sitting in trees preening or singing. I was enraptured. I would run back and forth along the path, sometimes held by my mother's hand, sometimes straining against it, sometimes listening to her voice as she directed my attention to something important. I can still sense today the sounds and smells and the mature greenery—flowers, ferns, trees, and foliage from other lands—that made it seem like a real jungle environment. Perhaps these experiences sparked my later interest in taking trips to Southeast Asian jungles, trekking and boating in the Amazon, hiking in the Himalayas, and going on safari in Africa.

If Eleanore had planted these seeds of adventure in me, I am forever grateful to her.

## EDUCATION

Eleanore taught me not only to read but also the names of flowers and birds (long forgotten) through cards designed for that purpose. We walked, and she talked, I hurrying to keep up with her longer legs. She enlisted others to teach me, once sending me to a two-week summer art class that I remember fondly. I learned to draw mountains with curvy lines across the top of the page, with a sun peeking out the top corner. I also learned to make things with rattan-like material in brilliant hues, a smell that stays with me today. Later, when I was visiting in Seattle, Washington, she sent me for elocution lessons, and I learned to say, "HO said the giant, IT IS I, I will BUILD you a CASTLE into the SKY." She provided me with violin lessons and sent me to a tap-dancing class on summer afternoons at the Central Elementary School. None of the lessons lasted long though. After she saw a tap-dance class in session once, she jerked me out of it. "That is silly," she said. Of all my experiences at the time, I loved tap dancing the most, and I still regret losing that opportunity to continue.

Living at home from the mid-1930s to the early '40s, I was a skinny, hyperactive, slightly dyslexic kid with an attention problem (what we would call an attention –deficit hyperactivity disorder, or ADHD, today) But to John Garmston I was scatterbrained. It was probably the ADHD along with behavior problems that landed me in a special education class when I was in the second grade. I took a city bus from our home in East San Diego to San Diego State University for the special class. Mostly I remember the small size of the class, sitting in rows, and some of my outrageous behaviors, like bellowing in class or falling on the floor if a student walking past happened to brush by me.

## LEAVING HOME

My "sojourns" from home started with my attending the special education class across town at age 7. It was a day school, and I am still astounded by the independence that was given me to get there. I took city buses and had to use transfer passes, then I walked to the university where the class was held.

Next there was the Busy Bee Group Home in Glendale, California. I was sent there twice, and the second time I was kicked out for bad behavior.

The Busy Bee was run by the Christian Science Church, and it seemed that the staff at the home didn't know any more about working with young children than the people who dealt with me later at Lytton. Two incidents at The Busy Bee stand out in memory. In one we were served an artichoke, which I had on good authority had a poisonous core. There was no way I was going to risk eating it. Had anyone thought to ask me why I didn't want to eat it, I would have said so and maybe the problem would have solved itself. But as it turned out, I was told to sit at the table until I ate the artichoke. I sat until the dining room was cleared, until the dishes were washed in the kitchen, until the staff went home to their beds, and still I sat there. Occasionally a part of me still sits at that table of memory, refusing to do what I think is wrong. In the second incident, I was disciplined and assigned to a single room (read "solitary") for three days, with only bread and milk to eat.

It was at the Busy Bee that I had my first thoughts of running away. Glendale lies about 12 miles inland from the Pacific Ocean, and I calculated that if I walked west to the ocean and then turned left toward San Diego, I could be home in a few days. On a map, this is a 116-mile journey. While my sense of direction was correct, the trip, for reasons that never occurred to me, was not feasible.

On reflection, I must have been a very difficult child to parent. Eleanore said I gave her a nervous breakdown. What a burden I must have been. I know I certainly failed to live up to her expectations, whatever those were. I was hyperactive, neglected chores, had fits of frustration, and could be well behaved or aggressive, cute or contemptible, moody or nice. In our house, the most common punishment I remember was being spanked with a wooden hanger by Eleanore as she held me over her lap and yelled how disrespectful, or selfish, or bad I was. Whenever the hanger broke, she went on screaming and grabbed another. John must have thought this was excessive, for once when I was threatened with the classic admonition "Just you wait until your father comes home," he took me into their bedroom, closed the door and told me to holler and cry while he beat the hanger against the bed.

Almost worse than the spankings was her lecturing me as a result of some supposed offense. Eleanore could drive me numb with words, words, words. I was to look at her and listen. Oh, how I hated those harangues. I became adept at reading the sign that one was coming—her pursed lips, with a slight downturn at the corners of her mouth.

She seemed to take delight in inflicting discomfort. Eleanore rubber-banded newspaper booties to our cat's paws and then laughed as the cat high stepped and struggled to scrape them off. I felt bad for the cat. On several occasions she got the family Chihuahua to cower and cry, tears running down its little face, by speaking harshly to her.

Eleanore's punishments, however, faded in comparison to John's. He delivered the two worst ones I remember ever receiving. Once when I had visited them in La Mesa, California, for Christmas, I was given a football and was ecstatic. I kept it with me all the time, throwing it up and down, even as I walked. One day it was missing. We searched everywhere for it, to no avail. When John drove me back to Lytton Home, where I was living at the time, he talked very little on the 10- or 12-hour drive up Highway 99. As he deposited me in front of my cottage at the home, he got my suitcase out of the trunk and said, "Oh, you will probably want this, too," handing me a scorched, partially burned football. Then he drove off. I stood frozen on the curb, charred football in my hand. Ashamed, angry, devastated, I had never felt so like a pile of shit than that afternoon in front of Sonoma Cottage. Our house on Morningside Drive had a furnace in the back yard. Apparently, when taking the trash out, I had put the football on top of the trash container as I walked and then, without realizing it, dumped the trash, football and all, into the furnace. I knew John's response to my losing the football was unjust and cruel. I was crushed, and his constant message to me was reinforced: I was a scatterbrained, ungrateful, no-good kid, and unloved.

The other "worst" experience with John was when he was scheduled to come to Lytton Home where I lived from 10 to 15 years of age. He was to pick me up so we could go on a two-week holiday together, maybe camping. I looked forward to this more than anything, for I lived in a constant state of wanting to be with my parents. It was summer, a lazy period of endless days with only occasional events to mark the time. Just before he came I did some bird-brained thing that got me in trouble with the home. John and the Lytton authorities decided that I couldn't go off with him. Worse, he wasn't even allowed to see me. I was inconsolable. I was angry with him for not fighting for me—and for my right to see him—and carried that anger for a long time.

This incident, like so many others, was reframed a few years ago. In letters revealed to me by Marabel Beck, my Lytton social worker, correspondence from John and Eleanore made it very clear they did not want me and that they even tried to reverse the adoption.

Eleanore often reminded me that I was adopted and that if I didn't behave she would return me to my real mother. Once she did this at the wharf while holding me over the railing at San Diego harbor. Crying, frightened and pleading with her to put me down on the deck, I promised to be good.

Eleanore gave birth to a baby girl when I was 7. This was about the same time that I was sent away to live at the Busy Bee Home in Glendale, California. When I was 12, Eleanore sent me a newspaper clipping of sister Lynne, now a kindergartner, crossing the street to go to school where they lived in San Diego. She was a cute little girl, blonde and striding purposefully across the street supported by a school crossing guard. I fantasized about being her older brother, protecting her from school bullies. We saw each other about 10 times growing up, each time for a week or two, and then had no contact until I returned from a two-year assignment in Saudi Arabia in 1972. I was 39. After our nearly 30-year separation, I am stunned by what she revealed. All that time I had thought Lynne was the lucky one, staying at home. All that time she thought I was. Lynne's life with Eleanore had mirrored mine, just with different accusations.

*Lynne and Eleanore*

Knowing now what I do about Lynne, maybe Eleanore's greatest gift to me was sending me away. Lynne told me that Eleanore was constantly telling Lynne that she was not wanted and that John had forced Eleanore to have her. She told my sister over and over again that Lynne had "ruined" her life. Lynne says that even when she was very young, she remembers thinking, 'That's not right—my mother should not be saying these things to me!'" [1]

The pressures Lynne felt when living with John and Eleanore were overwhelming. She describes one episode.

> "I remember really disappearing into a little dream world of my own. I would talk to myself, started doing strange things that I don't feel like talking about because I hardly remember but they were strange. I know and felt at that time that something was happening to me. One time I was having this imaginary dinner party with all my friends. I was all by myself, of course, and there was a window. It was a nice house with sort of a sunroom where I would like to talk to my friends. Mom and Dad were home then, and there was all this fighting,

throwing things, horrible language and all that. They were looking through the glass at me with a strange look on their faces like I was doing something really very weird. As far as I know at that time, all I was doing was talking to my little friends at the table, being a hostess at this grand dinner party. Then the next thing I know I was in a school that I later realized was a school for special children ... ."

I asked her, "Was it in Seattle where you told Eleanore that you would have as unhappy a life as she did, just to comfort her?" Lynne replied, "Yeah. We were with a bunch of other relatives on … a Sunday outing and Mom was crying, carrying on. We were with a couple of other people like Aunt Sarah, and Uncle Irving. I remember telling Mom she couldn't cry anymore because we did not have any more Kleenex. Then I told her not to worry, that I was going to have as unhappy a life as she had. I remember that so distinctly because at that time I was like 7 or 8 years old and knew it was a very strange thing for a 7- or 8-year-old to say to her mom. It is not right. When I got older

I thought I had to overcome that as it could become a pattern that I should guard against."

*Bob, Lynne and Eleanore*

While I had envied Lynne for living at home, her experiences were worse than mine in that from birth to about age 22 she had daily contact with and thoughtless emotional abuse from Eleanore. Her self-concept was shattered, and she remains today a bright but troubled person with an unfulfilled life.

I know it was from Eleanore that I developed a number of perceptions about myself, and it was probably from her that I got the notion that I looked sissified as a young child. For years I could not look at a picture of myself when young without feeling a sense of revulsion. I seemed to be what was wrong with our family and she what was right. She was unbelievably hard to live with for all of us. I learned much later that John (to his credit) had a mistress during the period when he served in Berlin during the German Air Lift. "Once a sailor, always a sailor," Eleanore would say afterward. I mentioned to Lynne that I thought tensions in the household were possible. "Tensions?" she said. "There were screaming fights, loud crying—this started in Seattle when John returned from Germany. It was at this time I believe I started retreating into my own world."

Before my reconnection with Lynne, my memory of Eleanore was of a woman who was trying to do the right thing. She told me often that she gave up nylons for me. She often presented herself in a heroic or martyred light. She said she married John to take care of me. Much later, after I had been sent away, I heard other stories from her, some hard to believe. In one, a woman who was accused in a murder plot, but never convicted, forced Eleanore to marry John. She could show me the news clipping if I wanted. My perception of Eleanore was that she had sacrificed parts of her life to take care of me. And at the same time, I knew that I was a worthless, very bad, unlovable boy.

Later in my 40s, I learned that Eleanore's behavior was not about me.

## FORGIVENESS

It's a sunny afternoon. The backyard lawn was recently mown and the smell of fresh grass is in the air. This is California, and the sky is predictably blue over Milpitas, near San Jose in the San Francisco Bay area. At the time, my second wife Mary and my adopted son Kevin lived here with me. I'm 43. This was the moment when I finally released myself from the destructive influence I had allowed my mother to have over me.

"You never get it together in life until you figure out that your parent's life was not about you." This was something I learned from Werner Earnhardt, the founder of the est seminar program popular in the

1970s and '80s ("est" in Latin means *to be*). So, with closed eyes on that fresh lawn in my back yard and openness of mind, I began an internal conversation with my mother. "Mom," I asked, "how was it for you when I was a child?" I was stunned by what followed. In a matter-of-fact voice, she said, "You know, I never did want to have children." Astonishingly, those nine words, in that very moment, released me! Released me from thinking that her pushing me away was about me. Released me from thinking the cause of my abandonment was me. Released me from my belief that the reason I was sent away was because I was the cause of her nervous breakdowns. Released me from thinking her dissatisfaction with my accomplishments was me. I suddenly had a glimmer of understanding, of her—and of myself. Werner said, "You love, and someone gets in the way." For Eleanore, unhappiness existed, and my sister and I got in the way. Later, with regret, I found that while my release from Eleanore's destructive influence was real, parts of that experience lived on in me and would need to be managed even later in my adult life.

Eleanore died nearly friendless and alone in Oakland, California, May 24, 1993.

# CHAPTER 3

*Oakland*

## BEGINNINGS

*Beginnings*

*ah*

*the papered peeling walls*

*that hold us yet*

*in adolescent shame*

*our egos maimed*

*the stench of old streets*

*and sagging wooden floors*

*lingering still from furtive eyes*

*that stole such peeks*

*into store windows*

*and rolling cars*

*and at people who walked*

## I Don't Do that Anymore

*with proud strides*

*assurance in their gate*

*or stealing a look*

*from dark streets into warm light*

*playing behind curtains*

*into  soft glows*

*playing along porches*

*of houses*

*we passed in the night*

*picturing a family*

*drawn about a dinner table*

*a father seated there*

*filling the air*

*perhaps*

*with smoke from a pipe*

*or so it seemed from books*

*of how the inner rooms*

*of such homes must feel*

*and look*

*and we passed on*

*into the night*

*pulling the games*

*about cars with one headlight*

*around our shoulders*

*like a cloak*

*warding off the fear*

*we went on into the night*

*cold and friendless*

*along the streets*

*afraid*

*—RJG*

After the Busy Bee Home I was sent to live with Aunt Violet in Oakland, California. This began a year in which I lived largely on the streets, sneaking home late at night to Violet's exasperation. From these experiences and later ones, running away from Lytton, a feral child lives within me and sometimes manifests himself in ways that surprise me.

What did I learn in the streets? Well, there were my clever cons, like having a "personal" telephone route. Every few days, I would stuff paper up the coin-return chutes of several public telephones and then later would make the rounds to remove the paper, collect the coins caught in there, and re-stuff the chutes. I hitchhiked up and down the length of California, hopped freight trains, shop-lifted, sneaked inside theaters to see movies for free, swiped beer out of Acme beer trucks that sat loaded for next day's deliveries on Wednesday and Friday nights and even swiped cookies from Mother's Cookies factory. I remember breaking and entering and causing wanton destruction to the Bella Vista Elementary School across the street from where I lived with Aunt Violet.

Later, running away from Lytton, I added to my repertoire: stealing cars, snatching purses, rolling a drunk, taking bikes, breaking and entering, leaving department stores with clean clothes over my dirty ones when I was on the run, nicking tips from restaurant counters in order to eat, robbing houses for food, removing cases of empty Coke bottles from behind liquor stores and then bringing them in the front door to get the deposit money for a bus fare to the next town. It was later that I learned to sniff gas, drink, smoke marijuana, use bennies and shoot up heroin—heroin only once, thank God, and it was circumstance, not strength of character, that saved me.

## LIVING WITH AUNT VIOLET

I had to pee. I remembered that this was my first night in Aunt Violet's house in Oakland. I remained in bed for a while, reconstructing the route to the bathroom: out the door from the room in which a cot had been set for me to sleep and then left into the hallway. I crept to the bathroom, opening and closing its door so as not to wake anyone. As I stood over the toilet, the release felt so good and I could hear the splatter into the bowl. Then, a strange sensation, warm like bathwater, began to move down my leg. In the morning, I discovered I had wet the bed.

This was Aunt Violet's introduction to me. Eleanore's older sister, she owned one of the tiniest houses I had ever seen. The front door opened right on the street, and nearly touching her house to the right was a neighborhood grocery store, also small. Directly across was the Bella Vista School, a red brick, three- story building and grounds taking up an entire block. It was there that I would spend nine months in a corner classroom on the third floor. Since my mother was having nervous breakdowns and trying to raise a baby, it seemed better that Aunt Violet would take care of me for a school year.

Squeezed inside eleven hundred square feet were a living room, a main bedroom, a second bedroom the size of three closets side to side where I was to sleep, and a porch area off the rear of the house for a wash tub and a kitchen. In the living room was a piano. And in the kitchen was Great-uncle Hans. He was an old man with Santa Claus hair and beard who lived with Violet. He walked with a shuffle, one foot brushing the ground and the other sliding forward, taking an eternity to move from room to room or go down the block in front of the house. On the kitchen table was a water glass with wine in it, a Bible, a Christian Science book and a pack of playing cards. The wooden table was covered with a red and white oilcloth. Under the dim lighting in the room, it must have been difficult for him to see as he alternated between reading the Bible with *Science and Health and Key to the Scriptures* by Mary Baker Eddy and playing solitaire. He spoke with an accent, which I later learned was Danish, but I can remember little more about him.

But I can remember my interactions with Aunt Violet, sometimes pleasant conversations, sometimes not as she raged at me about my behavior. On one occasion when I came home late at night after sneaking out my bedroom window, I opened the front door only to have a bucket of water come crashing down on top of me. She had built a ledge over the door so that when it was opened, the water, bucket and all, would plunge down on the unsuspecting entrant.

Aunt Babs, the youngest of Eleanore's sisters, came to live at Violet's while she was going to school at the University of California Berkeley. She was young, full of energy, and interested in fun and me. She moved on from Violet's when her husband, Bill, was discharged from the Army. Occasionally over the years, I would get a Christmas card from her. I had been fond of Babs and somewhere around my $60^{th}$ birthday wrote her a card, confessing that I had had a crush on her when she stayed with Violet. I was 9 or 10 then and she was probably in her early 20s, yet I was stricken in much the same way young girls fall in love with their teachers, or boys with a special adult figure. What she wrote back was startling.

Babs wrote that after the war, when she and her husband were getting settled in Oregon, they talked seriously of adopting me. They both cared for me, she wrote, saying that Bill had gotten to know me when visiting her at Violet's. What held them back, Babs wrote, is that they thought of me as exceptionally intelligent and were concerned they wouldn't be able to meet the needs of such a bright kid. My heart stopped on reading this. They had loved me enough to consider having me come live with them! How wonderful it might have been for me to know this at the time.

## THROUGH THE WINDOW

At Aunt Violet's I sneaked out often. My bedroom was in the back corner of the house on the side next to the grocery store. I would climb out my window and over a fence, dropping to the side near the store. This was before television occupied living rooms, and my choices were to stay at home and talk with Aunt Violet or stay in my room assembling model airplanes, which I hung from the ceiling. Outside were other kids in the night having adventures. I had become friends (or they tolerated me like a mascot, I'm not sure which) with a group of kids in junior high. I was still in sixth grade, a grade I was to repeat next year because of my young age, impressionable and eager to please, with way more guts than sense. A freight train corridor ran north and south not far from our neighborhood. We would hang around the freight yard many afternoons, picking up stuff and stealing things when we could. One time we found a military supply area where hundreds of rubber rafts were stored, along with a supply of K rations in each one. These were the World War II military field meals. I remember feeling somewhat guilty, wondering what would happen if one of the rafts had to be used by soldiers and there was nothing there to eat.

The best part of the experiences we had there was hopping on trains. There were two ways we got on. In the yards the trains went pretty slowly, as it took some time to pick up speed. We would sprint alongside a train and grab for the end ladder on a boxcar. The ladder would yank us along, and we'd feel the full power of the train. Then we'd pop a foot up onto the ladder and get on. Later we learned it was best to do this on the last car, where the ladder was behind the last set of wheels, so if we did happen to slip off there would be no danger from the following car. Once aboard, we could climb to the top of the boxcars and move from one to another—not like you see in the movies by jumping but by climbing down, balancing on the great metal coupling device between the cars, and then making our way up onto the other one. We rode on flatcars, inside boxcars, and on top of the trains.

We also had a way of getting on a train that was moving faster than we could run. We would run alongside as fast as we could, and after watching a car pass us we would get ready to lunge for the ladder on the next car. Then we would leap, grabbing the ladder with our two hands, and would pull our feet up until they were on the bottom rung. This, of course, was dangerous. One afternoon one of the kids missed the ladder as he lunged. His shoulder and head rolled underneath the train, but he was able to roll away before being hit and killed. This scared the hell out of us, and I think it probably changed our behavior for a full week.

Getting off the train was another challenge. We would have to wait until the cars were rolling slowly enough so we could jump off without hurting or killing ourselves. Trains would slow down at freight yards or on inclines or sometimes stop altogether in another freight yard. The movies show people jumping and rolling to break the fall. Maybe that is OK if a grassy slope is nearby, but we had to jump and hit the ground running alongside the train until we could catch our balance and slow down to stop. Once we couldn't get off until the train rolled the 40 miles into San Jose and stopped at the yards there. We had to hitch our way back home.

## HANGIN' WITH THE BOYS

It was later while living in Oakland that I learned I could not get drunk, or so I thought. The reality was that I couldn't drink enough beer to get a buzz on. Maybe this had more to do with how much beer I could get from the older boys than how much I drank. At any rate, I carried this impression with me when I went on to Lytton Home, where I was delighted to find that I could get drunk as a skunk on red wine while running around in the hills behind the home yelling, laughing and carrying on.

Oakland nights were for adventure. Evenings were often warm enough for shirtsleeves, and after sneaking out from Aunt Violet's house, I would join the older boys down the block and we would head out for some exploit. On Wednesday and Friday nights, the Acme Beer Company's trucks sat loaded for deliveries the next day. Acme was close to a movie house on Grand Avenue, and I remember that "My Wild Irish Rose" was playing there one evening. We sang scraps of the songs we knew from the movie as we planned our heist. Being the smallest of the group, they pushed me through a hole in the fence that protected the trucks. I would then hand out quart bottles of warm beer through the hole. We would take the beer back to our neighborhood, where a moving van was parked overnight on the street. Into the van went the beer. Then we scampered over the red brick wall surrounding Mother's Cookies factory, a few blocks from our homes, and made our way up the metal steps in the rear of the building to the huge room where cookies were being baked. As the big baking pans were removed from the giant ovens, we whisked hot cookies into paper sacks. The men who worked there tolerated these periodic ambushes and watched with amusement as we grabbed the cookies and then escaped. Back in the parked moving van, we feasted on cooling cookies and warm beer, telling stories and planning how to make pigeon raids in the next week or so.

Having pigeons as pets was a big deal to the older boys and another source of adventure for all of us. The hutches were outdoor/indoor cages made of lath, chicken wire and other scraps of abandoned wood. The outside surfaces gave some kind of protection from cold air so that pigeons that were tired after returning from their flights would not get sick. On one occasion, three of us walked to the Fruitvale area—I'm guessing about three miles south of our neighborhood, when rural sections were still part of the landscape. We crept past a three-story house and then sneaked into the barn behind it, where we stuffed pigeons into gunnysacks. As we were escaping, somewhere in the space between the house and the barn, a light went on in an upstairs room. A window was raised and a man began yelling at us. Caught in the act, we began running. Shots rang out! He was shooting! Running headlong across the property to get away, the three of us jumped into a drainage ditch, where we left the gunnysacks and pigeons in waist-deep water, and tore away, separating for safety. I didn't see the other boys again that night. I ran and ran and ran, until I finally got back to Aunt Violet's house, certain that one or both of the boys had been shot. Later, I thought sadly about those pigeons: They must have died. I never found out what happened to them but learned afterward that none of us had been hurt—each had found a way home.

This experience, of course, didn't stop us from looking for somebody else's pigeons. In the Lake Merritt area, near downtown Oakland, there were several old houses, multi-story structures that appeared mysterious and foreboding when it was dark out. We would find our way to the attics of some of them, our goal being to snatch pigeons off the roof. There I was, too small to reach from the attic window around the overhang of the roof to climb on top but light enough to be shoved through the window by older boys and then held while I got a grip on the overhang so I could pull myself up. I can't recall how I got the pigeons back into the attic—if, in fact, I ever did—but I do remember the absolute terror I felt in the midst of this foolhardy adventure.

Not everything we did, of course, was so dangerous. Shoplifting was relatively risk free, breaking into cars was easy, sneaking into movie houses was a lark, and the telephone scam involving jammed return chutes could be done with absolute safety. Oakland is bordered on one side by an estuary, and we would sometimes go there late at night to liberate small boats from their moorings and then paddle about under cover of darkness in the smelly waters.

Not everything we did was mischievous. In the most tragic event of my childhood, I was not looking to find trouble. I had fallen in love with a lost puppy, which, like puppies everywhere, was the embodiment of love with a capital L. He was tail wagging, face-licking, body-wiggling, innocent love, and he turned his attention totally on me. He became my reason for getting out of school at the end of the day. We would play together, wrestling on the front porch of a friend's house. I had known and loved him only a few days when he died.

Just a block over and down toward 14th Street, a major thoroughfare to Lake Merritt and downtown, a group of my friends were playing on the other side of the street. Excited about seeing them, I darted across the street, running to join the other boys. As I got near the sidewalk, I heard the screech of tires and a terrible whelp behind me. My puppy. Crying uncontrollably, I picked him up and brought him to the sidewalk. Because of me he was dead. I should have looked. I shouldn't have run. I shouldn't be so impulsive. My puppy was gone forever, the best thing in my life lost, because of me. Aunt Violet, of course, let me know that she thought so too, reinforcing my belief that I was scatterbrained, undependable, bad, a "boob," as John Garmston called me, and responsible for not only my mother's nervous breakdowns but everything bad around me. Even now, at 77, echoes of these thoughts sometimes rise above whispers in the background of my mind about my worth.

## INDEPENDENCE

The first time I cut school was when I was in sixth grade and living in Oakland. One gloomy, overcast day, two of us skipped school and headed for the streetcar tracks. We knew we could hop a car all the way to the edge of the hills bordering Oakland to the east. In those days, cowcatchers were still a part of a streetcar design, and we would run along a car as it accelerated from a stop, hop on the cowcatcher and hold on until we were discovered and chased off. If we were caught, we'd simply wait for the next car and do it all over again. At the end of the line, we jumped off, caught up in the joy of the adventure but hungry as well. So we began looking for something to eat. It wasn't hard to browse in a grocery store and then leave with a loaf of white Langendorf bread concealed under my jacket. But that was not enough.

We continued moving east, walking down the long, paved corridors of alleyways between houses, and before reaching our creek we discovered chickens in someone's back yard. We climbed the fence, grabbed a squawking, struggling chicken from the yard and then, back in the alley, swung it by the neck, as we had read about, until it was dead. Now we had bread and meat. In another alleyway a few blocks away we plucked the chicken, excited about being able to find food for ourselves. We talked and plucked, plucked and giggled, talked more and continued to pluck. To us, the job was not to get all the feathers and pinfeathers removed but to get most of them out as fast as possible so we could make a small fire and roast the bird. The chicken was half raw and half burned when we ate it, but still it was ours and a measure of my ability to survive on my own terms.

Heading east again, we reached the end of a housing project where there was a creek, swollen with rainwater. We picked our way along the gums of the stream, over rocks and logs, with the sounds of water cascading over the stones, through trapped foliage, bubbling up from miniature caves alongside. The sounds and movement were hypnotic. Leaves of yellow and gold and green moved swiftly on the water as it pooled here, cascaded over boulders there and, as with a life and will of its own, kept moving downstream. To this day, streams are for me a symbol of freedom, adventure, wonder and timelessness.

When I was not hanging out with older kids, or hanging from the monkey bars at the school across the street from Violet's, or off in the dark on some adventure, my aunt and I would dress in our Sunday best and walk the mile or so to the Christian Science church at Lake Merritt. I had lessons to do before each Sunday came around, and then I enjoyed the walk, the time with Violet and the serious, reasoning tone of the services.

In addition to taking me to church, she arranged for me to take piano lessons, and I enjoyed being able to play a couple of beginner's tunes on the piano at her house. Like the few violin lessons that Eleanore had provided for me before I left San Diego, the piano lessons did not last long, but I am grateful even today that I was able to play these instruments as much as I did.

I left Aunt Violet's at the end of a school year to repeat sixth grade at a new location. A wonderful opportunity had opened; I was told, for me to attend a home for boys and girls for the summer. I never saw my aunt again.

# CHAPTER 4

## *This Was Not a Sunday School*

*Overheard at a Starbucks*

*"The counselors are limiting my access to Jesse. I can only email once a week and no phone calls. What if he gets sick, or has a falling out with his friends, or is hurt?" she said.*

*"Let it be. The first time away from mom is a huge opportunity. They learn things not possible at home—like independence and taking care of yourself no matter what comes up," he answered.*

I listened and smiled when I heard the above exchange. I had never thought about what I learned by being away from home with a pack of loosely supervised kids, first at The Busy Bee Home in Glendale, then to Oakland with Aunt Violet and then for five years at Lytton Home, an institution that was located about 100 miles north of San Francisco. Who I am today, in part, has been shaped by my experiences there.

With Eleanore's approval, I was sent to Lytton for five years. This was another lie my parents told me and one in which Violet conspired—that I was going to a nice place for the summer. I was 10. Since I knew it was a home run by the Salvation Army, I resolved to quit smoking, drinking, and swearing. What a joke. Most of the kids there were wards of the court, some there as an alternative to juvenile detention, some because their families could not care for them. The residents included 130 children, 100 boys and 30 girls. It was directed by a Salvation Army major and run by deans, kitchen staff, hospital staff, cottage mothers, and maintenance crew. A social worker was on the staff. The kids were the custodians.

My first response to Lytton was to be wary, sometimes scared but almost always wary.

Far from its being a Sunday school, it was, I learned, a place where many of the kids had more "colorful" backgrounds than mine. Smoking and swearing were taken for granted. Lytton kids came from broken homes; many had spent time in juvenile detention facilities because their parents couldn't care for them, or they were there because of burglary, gang activity, and petty theft. Some had been sexually molested by parents, as had happened to my future wife, Irene. Some were children of migrant farm workers; some had been taken from their homes due to neglect; and some came from a sprinkling of families like mine whose parents were willing to pay a monthly fee to have their offspring cared for by someone else. This would be my peer group, my tutors, my friends and my enemies for five developmental years.

Salvation Army officers were the chiefs at Lytton. Major Taylor was the Lytton superintendent when I arrived. Those in the supervisory positions—deans and cottage mothers—were not paid much, nor were they required to have any certification or educational credentials. As a result, some were hired from the bottom of the labor pool. It was revealed later that two, after leaving the home, were arrested for pedophilia. Knowing this reframed my experiences with one of the men. One was a sadist; another had an anger management problem. One smelled like a cigarette factory but was a pretty good guy. I'll talk about them later, in particular a former military man whose attitude about authority did a lot to develop mine.

The social fabric of life at Lytton was, I suppose, not unusual whenever you have a group of kids living together. Given the reason why some of them had been placed there, the times of the "sentences" varied, for that is how many of us thought of our stay there. Two of them, for example, had arrived as preschoolers. Many had at least a three- or four-year stay; few were in and out in a short time. Supervision was limited, for there was too much acreage to cover as well as too few staff. The environment often felt unsafe; in fact, it was not a place where you could really let your guard down. There was some bullying, and some kids could be quite vindictive, carrying grudges for long periods of time. I learned to step aside for them.

## TO CAMP

Our whole group, about 130 of us, was bussed each year to summer camp in the Mendocino Woodlands, a 700-acre park nestled among groves of redwood trees, ferns and open spaces just off California's rugged north coast. Lying along both sides of the north fork of the Big River, the entire park has since been designated a national historic landmark by the U.S. Department of Interior. There are hiking trails in the park as well as open meadows and a large beaver pond populated with river otters, and deer, fox and other animals. At one point along the river, a big diving board extended from a rocky outcropping. We would walk there to enjoy the sun, the deep water and the sand on the other bank.

In this idyllic setting, kids were assigned to cabins—each containing two bunk beds, a closet, a bathroom and a back porch overlooking a meadow or tiny creek. The rustic cabins were spread out along forest paths, well-trodden and littered with redwood needles that needed to be swept each morning by the cabins' inhabitants. The cabins were placed mostly in view of one another, except ours, cabin 41, the last one, which was located in an isolated spot.

Without doubt, cabin 41 was the premier lodging. There was a small creek that ran below it where tadpoles and very tiny fish could be found. We "fished" using string, tiny hooks and white bread molded into diminutive squares. Those of us who were placed there seemed to be allowed an unusual degree of independence and a delicious absence of adult supervision. Other kids knew that, of course, and even the deans must have known. But, by chance, four of us newbies—we had been at Lytton for less than a week—were assigned to this most desirable piece of real estate. Other kids were pissed, and the "old timers" among them were incensed at this injustice, some feeling downright vindictive.

## BEING THE NEW KID

I remember two of the newbies now but not the third. Richard (Hammie) and Eugene were brothers from logging country somewhere up north. They wore steel-toed boots and told stories, in uneven grammar, about men who had their toes chopped off cutting wood. Physically strong with limpid blue eyes, Hammie was the older of the two brothers and walked ever so slightly off center so that he would unintentionally nudge walking companions to the side of roads. Eugene was about my age. (Hammie joined the Navy after he aged out of Lytton, becoming a kind of a pathetic model for my highest aspirations. Later we learned that after he returned from his service in the Navy, he was killed in a logging accident.)

The cabin 41 kids knew fear, twice a week as regular as the calendar. As unwitting residents of the most desired cabin, we were systematically set upon after amphitheater events. The amphitheater was where the kids performed skits. It was constructed of logs, which were arranged in terraced fashion on three sides of the arena, leaving the fourth side open for a makeshift stage. On Sunday and Wednesday nights the group watched performances and sang songs, and, as darkness fell the melancholy sounds of taps could be heard emanating from the hillsides.

The walk from the amphitheater back to our cabin was long, dark, and perilous. Towering redwoods blocked our access to the night sky. We never knew from which direction an attack would come or when; only that it would come at some point along the path. Shouting wildly and brandishing clubs, kids would jump us, raining blows on us with sticks and fists and feet for what seemed like an eternity. Afraid and angry and disgusted by my own submissiveness, I would stand there with my nose running and tears flowing until the assailants would leave us in the woods as they disappeared into the night. The darkness, pitch black under the forest canopy, made it impossible for us to see our attackers or know where to run to escape. I was later to learn, however, that adults could be more dangerous than kids.

## FEAR IS A FICKLE FRIEND

Fear, of course, helps one survive, although too much of it can slow or shut down one's ability to think for a time. I became super alert at Lytton as a result of the forest beatings. When I ran away from the home, as I did on more than one occasion, I would walk on dark San Francisco streets gripping an open pocketknife in my pocket. I had heard that gangs would jump a kid and try on his shoes, but if they didn't fit, one member of the gang would shred them with razor-sharp knives. I doubt, however, that I would have had the guts to use my pocketknife if I was ever attacked.

At Lytton I was also afraid of some of the older kids, those who would take whatever they wanted unless I could be cunning enough to distract them or cover up my fear. On run-away adventures I was, of course, afraid of being spotted by cops and sometimes felt apprehensive when people who were out and about were paying too much attention to me. Stealing, I knew what it was like to be anxious—I would have been crazy not to feel this— and I remained fearful of, and even angry at, authority even into my adult life.

Sometimes fear complicates survival. Today, I experience different kinds of fear—fear of failure, of not being good enough, of being an imposter, of being excluded, of not being accepted, of the unknown, or of what might lie on dark streets in cities in which I travel for my work. I drive my wife nuts by exclaiming, "There's a cop" whenever we are driving; to her, it's no big deal, but for me it's a reminder to be cautious.

I envy my friends who seem unaffected in the presence of authority. While I have graduated from this degree of being incapacitated, I still feel ill at ease when I'm with a person whose authority I respect. I lose my social graces and what I know about the topic we discuss. I trembled, for God's sake, when speaking to an officer in the Navy.

## OH, YOU POOR CHILD

Sonoma Cottage was to be my home for the full five years at Lytton, and cottage mothers came and went. Three more cottages—Sequoia, Sotoyome and Oaks—housed the other boys. The "Big House," the main structure at the top of a slight rise, held the dining hall, kitchen, laundry, administrative offices and, on the second floor, accommodations for about 30 girls.

I heard "Oh, you poor child" many times from cottage mothers where I was housed with about 24 other boys. "Ma" Pierson was a middle-aged or maybe even older woman whose living quarters were located just off the front entrance in a tiny apartment adjacent to the main living room. Her duties were to supervise, though I am not clear what that entailed. Sometimes I thought her main job was to argue with me about the date of my birth. For more than a year I carried on an argument with her over when I was born. Was it the $24^{th}$ or $26^{th}$ of the month? I remember this being significant because 12-year-olds could stay up an hour later and I wanted to be 12 as soon as possible. I recall, too, being admonished by one of the cottage mothers to "comb our hairs" before going to the dining hall—an expression that never failed to draw titters, a response I'm sure she didn't understand. For us, "hairs" referred, of course, to pubic hair, a topic of amusement to budding adolescents, and "hair" was what grows on top of one's head. Ma broke up fights, gave the lights out signal and made sure we cleaned up the cottage every day. At night, the dean on duty would peer into the two wings of the cottage and then leave silently, as if he or she had not been there at all.

The thing that got me about the "poor child" comment was that it was never clear to me what those who said it about me were talking about. Whatever I was experiencing seemed normal to me. My life was regimented: eating in the dining hall, working on assignments, going back to the dining hall, maybe walking to the Russian River on summer afternoons, heading back to the dining hall, playing kick the can or other games into the twilight, having some quiet time, and then heading to bed. It was the same thing the next day, unless we had an afternoon free when some of us went into the hills behind Lytton for an adventure. Sundays meant church, where we could sing and listen to fire-and-brimstone preachers— often visitors

*L*

*ne*

from the outside—who would tell us how they used to smoke cigars and drink until they found Jesus.

During the school year, I attended William Booth School, located on the facility's grounds. After graduation from the eighth grade, we were bused to Healdsburg High School in town, which gave us a break from our daily routines.

I began at Lytton in the summer of 1945 and repeated sixth grade in the fall. During that year, a teacher discovered that I did not know my alphabet and kept me after school until I could recite it. I still have a sense of delayed development when looking things up. Over the years I've compensated for this in a variety of ways, asking someone else to do this when possible.

# CHAPTER 5

## *Dangerous Adults*

Rusty, not his real name, came when I was in my third or fourth year at Lytton. He seemed huge to us kids, especially the younger ones. He loomed over us and walked like a cocky military man, talked like one and barked like one. His charges in Oaks Cottage would "stand for inspection" each day, as he stood in front of the first in line, and bellow, "What cottage are you in?" "Oaks Cottage, SIR," his diminutive charge would respond. In response to the question "Why?" the kid would reply, "Because we're the best, SIR," punching out the word "sir" with all his developing lungs could muster. Twenty or so boys, ages ranging from 8 to 16, stood in a line and were backed up against a wall in the dingy hallway. His big belly seemed to close the distance if their response was not quick enough or loud enough. Kid by kid, he worked his way down the line, like a drill sergeant inspecting his troops. He had a military-style haircut, wore work boots, and walked with an attitude that said "I am the man here and don't you dare mess with me."

Rusty seemed to be disliked and feared by kids from the time he arrived at Lytton. "Hated" is the better word for me, since he seemed to be the embodiment of all that was bad, frightening and inappropriate about authority. I was to have my encounter with him soon after he arrived.

He had been hired as a "housemother," but I cannot understand what possibly was going on in the minds of Lytton authorities when they hired him. He was trouble with a capital T, destined to cause controversy, injury and possibly a lawsuit to the home.

## MESSING WITH RUSTY

One hot day after Rusty had been at the home for a couple of weeks, a stake-bed truck felt its way cautiously down the rutted road, hauling dozens of dusty, sweat-streaked boys to their work projects on the Lytton property. Rusty drove. No one really knew much about him other than he was big and claimed to have been a Marine. Several of the more daring kids delighted in jumping off the truck, running behind it for a few yards and then jumping back on. Rusty bellowed for us to stop. We didn't. Suddenly, the truck lurched to a stop, and he came stomping out of the cab, mad as hell. "OK," he yelled, "who's been jumping off the truck after I told you not to?"

I was cocky and skinny. My ribs showed through my skin whenever I wore a swimming suit. Some times I showed little sense. I stood a few feet from the end of the truck, a piss ant to his giant cockroach, and in a *who are you to tell me what to do voice* said, "I was!"

Without another word, he reached for one of my legs and yanked me off the truck. Surprised, and with the wind knocked out of me, I lay on my back in the summer dirt. To be sure his lesson was clear, he began to kick me over and over again. I can't recall if I cried, but I know I pivoted on my back to avoid his kicks, the way one would fight off an attacking dog, and I remember that I hated him at that moment. If his message was that he was in charge, what he says goes, and don't ever, ever give him shit, my response was not what he would have intended. Fuck you, Rusty. You will not rule me, I thought.

Most of my interactions with the staff that looked after us were not as traumatic. At times, adults could find me easy to get along with and likable. One of them who loved to fish would organize fishing trips for some of the boys. Another one would talk to us about our interests. He was instrumental in the construction of a darkroom at the facility, and I loved taking pictures and working to develop them there afterward. I'm pretty sure the postcard of Lytton as a school home for boys and girls was taken by me. I have the original. But then there was the one who would take walks with some of us into the wooded hills behind the property, unobtrusively slipping his hand down the back of our Levis to put his hand on our asses. Although at the time I didn't think anything about it, he was later arrested in San Diego and charged with pedophilia.

Another dean, in an act of moral courage and kindness, came to Sonoma Cottage one night, woke me and my best friend Gilbert from a sound sleep and directed us to the bathroom. There he whispered a warning to us, swearing us to secrecy in the dimly lit room as we stood between the washbasins and urinals. There was a plot against us, he said; some of the other deans wanted to drive us away from the home because they were sick and tired of dealing with the two of us. He said they had resolved that if we ran away one more time they would have us sent to Preston, the boy's reformatory at Ione, somewhere in the California Gold Country. Preston was where the hard cases—boys our age up to 20—were sent. To be sure that would happen, he said, they would make it as hard on us as possible, giving us shit details and leaning on us whenever they could.

Shortly after that, Gilbert and I were told to remove grape vines from the vineyard in the center of the property. It was hard, exhausting work, but we *Yes, sir*-ed them to death, the bastards who made us do it. We were going to beat them at their own game.

As it turned out getting in trouble did cause me to leave Lytton, but under better circumstances.

> On a recent weekend getaway, my wife and I found ourselves meandering about the Sierra Nevada foothills near Sacramento. Quite accidentally we stumbled on the town of Ione. In the distance, we could see towers and thought we might be seeing church spires. As

> we navigated the town's narrow street and then climbed a small rise, the old reform school came into view. I could see the place where we would have been sent. The old building had been vacated in 1960, a year, coincidentally, after the closing of Lytton Home. This, I surmised, would have been our residence had the deans been successful in forcing us out.

## WELCOME BACK SHOWER

There were two other incidents with deans that are indelibly inscribed in my memory and that colored my impression of authority. "Oh, you must be glad to be back after running away from the home," he said in a saccharine voice. "I'll bet you got awful dirty hitchhiking and sleeping on the ground. I bet you would appreciate a nice clean shower to freshen up after your adventures."

This was Ted, not his real name, another big man but one with a quiet air of complete authority. He had been at the home for many years before I arrived. He was the king of deans; others afforded him the courtesy of taking his lead in situations.

"Oh, you must want to get clean" was a standard conversation starter that a returning run-away heard. Once he held a 14-year-old boy firmly by the elbow and walked him to the gym and into the shower room, where the boy was made to strip and step under the water. Using a scrub brush with stiff bristles, he scrubbed the boy with the vigor and thoroughness of an apprentice swabbing a deck, removing all traces of "runaway dirt." This happened during my first week at the home, and I remember seeing the boy after his coming-home shower. His face was raw from the scrubbing. This was my introduction to Lytton discipline, and it was only later that I learned that even though the dean had given the boy a vigorous scrubbing the boy had gone into the shower just as he had entered Lytton, with a pockmarked face. But first impressions are hard to overcome.

## I'M GOING TO KILL YOU

My other significant encounter with a dean was much worse. Rumors that one of the deans, lets call him Clay, had played football were probably due to the fact that he looked like a linebacker. He had a short fuse, and I accidentally set it off one day.

To go to meals, the boys lined up under a covered space right outside the dining hall, and the girls entered from inside the big house so they were at another side of the dining hall. As each cottage would form a line, I stood in the Sonoma Cottage group. For each of us, the goal was to get as close to the front of the line as possible so that when our cottage was called to enter we could race to our designated table and the first could yell, "First and first extras!" The second person to be seated would shout, "Second and second extras!" And so on.

Meals were served family style. We didn't have much opportunity for seconds in the main dish, but there was always an unlimited supply of milk. Gilbert and I got pretty good at being first or second to the table so we could take command of the milk. We would drink it without letting go of the pitcher and then pour another glass, repeating this until the pitcher was empty. If one of my friends was first, he would hand the empty pitcher to me, so I could take it to the kitchen and have it refilled before returning to the table to do what he had done. When I was finished, I would hand the pitcher off to someone else. Mealtime would often end before the fifth or sixth kid at the table could get any milk! If second helpings were left on the platter or another platter was delivered to our table, the "first and first extra" kid would be assured of seconds because he was the earliest to the table and so the soonest to recite the magic words. Even today I feel compelled to be the first in any line—in airports, shopping lines, car lanes—and also eat too fast.

Dessert was the focus of another mealtime ritual. It could be bartered for. I *really* like tapioca pudding, for example, and would promise someone two desserts later in exchange for some kid's pudding today.

Leaving the dining hall one day, I got into trouble with Clay. After breakfast, we would line up so he could dismiss us according to the order of the day's work projects. Every boy had a job, some larger than others. As payment for our work, we received script that could be spent at a closet-sized candy store next to the gym that was open on Saturday mornings. Some jobs paid 10 cents a week, others 25 cents. If a kid happened to be industrious, he could line up several jobs and have up to 50 or 60 cents to spend on Saturday.

Clay was announcing the names of the kids who were to be released to work and dismissed the boys on cottage duty. This was not my assignment, but I walked away from the line anyway. I hadn't gotten far before he yelled out to me, telling me that he knew I was not part of that work crew, and ordered me back to the line. I remember a flush rushing over my body, and although I was angry, it would have been better not to respond. But there was something in his tone that just pissed me off, so I said something back. "Don't lip off to me!" he yelled, and when I responded in kind, even using his intonation, he exploded and lunged for me. I was standing several paces away in a graveled courtyard and turned to run. It was difficult to get any traction, which made me even more afraid. I managed to round the corner of the big house and head down across a lawn, but he was close behind me and getting closer. At that moment occurred one of those incidents that bound Gilbert, my closest of friends, and me inextricably closer. Although it seemed he didn't have enough weight, he threw a body block at the dean's legs, knocking him down. Clay, swearing like a stevedore, got up and tore after me again. Even though I had gained several yards on him, I was still at a disadvantage because he was so much bigger, and he finally caught me, in front of Sequoia cottage. When he grabbed me by the shoulders and pulled me toward him, I had no doubt in my mind that he wanted to kill me.

I managed to break free and, in full fright, ran back up the hill toward the big house, Clay right behind me. I barged into the superintendent's office and went behind his desk, and, thankfully, when Clay entered after me, his superior stopped him. My mind is blank as to what happened next. I can only imagine that I was made to apologize, and I am sure that I did, because at that point I would have probably been willing to apologize for the Lindberg kidnapping or anything else if it would calm my chaser and get him far, far away from me.

## IT'S NOT OVER

There was more to the incident, however. One night, another dean roused Gilbert from a sound sleep and walked him up the hill toward the enclosed swimming pool and into the dark of the maintenance yard. Even though my bed was next to his, I didn't hear anything, but Gilbert later told me that he was slapped around, to pound some sense into his head.

He knew the game, how to play dumb and when to be compliant if he needed to, for he had had lots of practice with San Francisco cops before he arrived at Lytton.

It still wasn't over. To get a sense of what happened next on another night, imagine our dormitory in the shape of a shoebox. At one end are lockers as well as a door going into the living room and another turning right into the bathrooms. At the back is a wall. Along each side of the room are cots, about six to a side. My cot was in the corner against the far wall, next to my friend's. The outer clothes we had worn that day were on the floor between our beds. Going to bed, we would kick off our dirty Levis, stow our shoes and socks under the bed, and cast our T-shirt on top of the Levis.

On the night Clay entered, it was after lights out and I was smoking in bed. I began to sense a presence standing in the shadows of the doorway to the living room. I knew he was on duty that night and, terrified, closed my fist around my cigarette, crushing it out in the palm of my hand. I stayed still in bed, trying to control my breathing as I strained to see into the shadowed darkness. Nothing moved, yet someone was there. Then a shape, with slow, soundless steps, moved from the doorway to the side of my bed. "Get up," he whispered. "Put your clothes on."

As I s-l-o-w-l-y got dressed, I tried to find a way to wake my buddy. Alone in the dark with no witnesses, I had to followed Clay outdoors. We turned left toward Oaks Cottage, the last of the houses lodging the boys, and walked silently in the pitch darkness until finally, halfway between the cottages, in the dark, we stopped. He stared at me ominously and then snarled, "You are one lucky son of a bitch. If you had made one God-dammed comment tonight—one back talk—I would have beat the shit out of you." With that, he turned and headed back in the direction of my dorm, and I followed on shaking legs. It's terrible to feel so powerless in such a perilous situation, and this was an experience that probably lives inside my DNA like no other.

I had other experiences at Lytton that were pleasant. I like to think of them as the modern boy's (by 1940s' standards), delightful journey of childhood.

# CHAPTER 6

## *Escapes*

Despite the challenges I encountered there, Lytton was a better place for me to be than at my mother's home. Perhaps the best parts of my Lytton experiences were the many avenues of escape, either through games, "boy" projects, running-away adventures, or even just meandering through the wooded hills behind the facility. In addition to those escapes, I formed positive relationships with three adults that were significant in my development, and one of them redirected me from the path I was on.

Lytton Home sat at the intersection of Lytton Springs Road and U.S. Route 101, midway between Healdsburg and Geyserville. Railroad tracks ran along side and parallel to The 101, and it was here we could hop on slow-moving trains and let them take us to awaiting adventures. It was also here that we learned to "walk the tracks," sometimes as far as

Geyserville, seven miles away. There was a life lesson to be learned here, though I didn't understand it until my 30s. It was important to look down the tracks, not at your feet, for when looking at the "goal" you don't fall off as easily.

Service trucks leaving Lytton and heading north on The 101 stopped before entering the highway, and as they started accelerating, we could hop on the back. Sometimes we were thrown off, but sometimes we just jumped off a few yards down the highway.

Geyserville at that time still had wooden sidewalks along its two blocks of town along the highway. The town boasted of a soda fountain, where one of the kids from Lytton and I sat one day. JT ordered a chocolate milkshake, and I was surprised when he got upset watching the man put vanilla ice cream into the container while making it. He had been at Lytton since the age of 5 and had never had a milkshake or seen one being made before. He didn't realize that the vanilla ice cream went in first and was followed by chocolate sauce.

The highway was a great source of cigarette butts. Fairly regularly I would go there, sometimes with another kid, and bring back smoke-able cigarettes. That was before I graduated to ninth grade, which meant I could go into town, where I would steal cartons of Camels from the Safeway store. Cigarettes became a measure of wealth at the home and would sometimes lead to cigarette wars.

Lytton Springs Road, then called the county road, bordered the northern edge of the property. Across the county road near the highway was an apple orchard. Farther north sprawled seemingly endless hills covered with California grasses that turned gray in summer and were tall and lushly green in winter. There were oak, laurel, and Manzanita on the property, and in the creeks were blackberries, poison oak and wild grapes, whose vines extended high into the trees and were sturdy enough for us to swing like Tarzan across the rain-swollen creek in the winter. My daughter Judy and I visited this place recently and saw dirt trails that are as wide as roads, extending far into the backcountry. I don't remember the trails being that wide when I was a kid, but if those roads did exist then, I'll bet they were there to access the mineral springs hidden in the deeper hills. Kids would find old bottles up there—evidence that at one time someone had been bottling, labeling and selling the water from the springs.

We would go northward in the hills, maybe a couple of miles or so, toward Geyserville to a farm we used to call the hermit's place. Looking down from the hills we could see, besides the vineyards and farm equipment, the large barn where we would make periodic raids. Inside, the owner kept gallons of red wine that he had made, and we would grab a couple of bottles and then run crazily around the hills, drunk from the wine and on life.

Always searching for ways to alter consciousness, we even tried applying pressure to the carotid artery until we passed out. We also mixed aspirin with water from a seltzer spring on the property, which never did much for me. Choking each other was more effective than the drinks we mixed. My guess is that this was more or less normal behavior for adolescent boys who want to test and go beyond the boundaries of sensation. Later, when I was allowed to work at a dairy farm, I learned to drape my arms over a 50-gallon tank of gasoline and, with my nose inserted at the blow hole in the top, inhale the fumes so I could watch electric sparks circulate in my head.

## FALLING DOWN, PASSING OUT DRUNK

Wanting to alter my consciousness didn't stop there. One afternoon two sophomore classmates and I cut school and went to a woman's house in town. I guess one of the boys was seeing her on a regular basis, but at the time no such thoughts occurred to me. We all sat and talked and sipped Four Roses whisky, my first taste of hard liquor, and I remember the warmth that spread through my body. This was good stuff. Being good, of course, meant that I wanted more, so I took the bottle into the bathroom to get more than my share. At some point, I passed out. The woman woke me later, saying her husband was coming home. I had to get out.

I can recall stumbling, weaving, being falling-down drunk yet determined to walk to the home, some seven or eight miles away. The next thing I can remember is lying on The 101, with cars stopped on both sides of the highway. "Are you all right?" anxious adults asked me. I mumbled that yes, I was fine; I had just lain down for a nap. Afterward, I stumbled into the apple orchard and fell unconscious again. I have no idea how I got back to Lytton that night, how my absence was explained, nor what consequences there were. Later in life, however, I learned to appreciate hangovers almost as much as the drunk, partially for their numbing affect. Perhaps that is what happened on this occasion—my memory was numbed into oblivion.

Today I realize that this event foreshadowed a direction in which my life would turn. I was nearly 40 and had experienced damaged relationships and job prospects before I learned that some people have a genetic predisposition to alcohol. We become incapable of turning away from drink on the basis of will power alone. But back then, when I was a high school sophomore, drinking could lead to embarrassment but was also an adventure. The first of many.

## HEALTHIER ADVENTURES

The hills behind Lytton were our best playground. We fashioned heavy cardboard and corrugated pieces of tin into sleds. In the summer, we would lift the lowest stands of the barbed-wired fence at the bottom of the hill so we could slide as far as possible on the dry grass. This was fun until one day a kid got his neck caught in the barbed wire as his sled kept right on going toward the county road. Like the accident at the freight yards in Oakland, this stopped us for a while.

We played for hours on a giant bay tree just across Lytton Springs Road. Sprawling branches went this way and that, like a friendly octopus. We could shimmy, climb, hop, hang and even play tag there. I was surprised a couple of years ago when I was preparing for hip surgery to find that this tree, which we called the "monkey tree," came involuntarily to mind as a "safe place" as I attempted to meditate.

## MONKEY TREE

*hello old tree*

*coiled as my memories*

*expansive limbs*

*twisted and gnarled*

*a haven for the careful*

*feet of climbing boys*

*can you remember*

*the fear in my thighs*

*locked so tight around you*

*my seat*

*inching upon your back*

*or was i just another*

*indistinguishable from all*

*the rest who played*

*and called*

*who crept and leapt*

*along your byways?*

*your sturdy trunk*

*has grown a hide of moss*

*today no boys surround you*

*or slide their jeans*

*along your form*

*i remember where*

*i used to put my feet*

*remember reaching*

*for a leap*

*to that branch there*

*where not every one*

*would dare to go*

*—RJG*

One memorable winter, Gilbert, another kid and I stole empty potato sacks from the kitchen. At a narrowing of a creek, we filled them like sand bags and carefully lined them up to create a backwater under the slender bay trees. Huge vines dropped from the trees, and we would swing there, from one side of the creek, dropping onto the muddy banks on the other side.

Once when heavy rains threatened our dam we ran into the hills to save our structure. Other kids had beaten us there and destroyed parts of what we had constructed, but we were determined to save the dam. We navigated the slippery mud on the banks until we could stand chest deep in the water, getting more potato sacks in place and trying to repair the breaks that kept appearing in the dam. We were better at building a dam than repairing one, yet it was fun. Finally, with blue lips and shivering bodies from the cold, we abandoned the project and returned to the home.

Where were the adults on all these occasions? Weren't we ever missed? We had a freedom that many kids today might not have. Who, for example, wouldn't want to have a tree house? Gilbert and I led the building of two tree houses. One was pretty rough by tree-house standards. Wooden steps were nailed to the trunk of a tree trunk across from the apple orchard down near the highway, and odd pieces of wood and cardboard were propped up or nailed in the crotch of the tree. Several of us went there afterward to do what boys do—argue, take sides, and tell stories.

The second tree house was much better and was hidden away high in the hills behind Lytton. To build our masterpiece, we took hammers, saws, nails and lumber from the maintenance department at the home, and we pirated two by fours and sheets of plywood. Getting the wood to our tree house site required a lot of effort and time. We needed to sneak the building materials away from adult eyes and stash them near the county road. On another trip, we would hustle the materials across the road, up past the monkey tree, and along a gradually ascending path that led to a natural saddle in the hills. The hardest work was getting the stuff up and over the steep hills to where we had selected the building site.

To a boy's eyes, the tree house was a marvel of construction, with fresh wood, squared sides, an actual roof, and an open framed doorway. We spent many hours there, refining the structure, talking about girls, sharing fantasies and stories. We talked about running away, planned run-aways and reminisced about past times we had left the home. We always talked about how we had gotten caught and what we could do to keep it from happening "the next time." We plotted ways to get even with kids who had wronged us, maybe by stealing their cigarettes. If ever there was a Huck Finn or Tom Sawyer part of my life, perhaps precious chunks of it were spent running away as well as there in the tree house, a lovely refuge away from adults.

## CIGARETTE WARS

Memories of our cigarette wars surfaced on a recent trip. My wife and I were driving south on The 101 from Ukiah, where my daughter Kimberly and her family live, and down to Santa Rosa, where we stopped for lunch. The route, through Hopland, wound along the Russian River as it snaked and cascaded its way past Squaw Rock and into Cloverdale, where Highway 128, a two-lane rural road, veers off to the west, toward Boonville and the coast. The old bridge at Cloverdale is gone now, as is the swimming hole below it where, as kids, we were brought occasionally to swim, a few of us sneaking up the cliff to break into the small store at its crest. To have packs of cigarettes, along with candy and Cokes, which were consumed on the spot, made us feel unbelievably rich. We considered ourselves adventurous, not bad.

For a while cigarettes were our treasure. Later they were the reason for the wars in the cottage where we lived. Gilbert and I delighted in considering ourselves the cleverest, most daring and most ruthless of the smoke thieves. Once after we stole two packs from the locker of a boy who could beat us up with one hand tied behind his back, we went into the common room to ask him for a cigarette. When he went to his locker to get it for us, we laughed and claimed we had been robbed too. That was the first time that we buried several cartons of shoplifted smokes and ones we had stolen from other kids behind our cottage.

## FIRE!

Adventure was often at hand; you just needed to look for it. Sometimes it found you.

"Fire, fire!" we screamed, tumbling over the steam pipes at the back of the cottages and running around to the front where we could be seen. "Fire! Fire at the school!"

We were successful, three of us, in alerting the community. Dry grass and then oak trees had caught fire at the back of the school. Flames nibbled at the roof. Kids and men with equipment rushed up the hill to the school. They used blankets to beat the grass fire down and hoses to extinguish the flames lapping at the trees and roof. The fire was eventually brought under control, and to my knowledge no one knows who started it.

No one, that is, except me, Gilbert and Jack. We were lighting kitchen matches, throwing them in the grass and then, at just the right moment before the fire got too large, stamped the flames out. That was the game, and it got out of hand. Gilbert and I blamed Jack for starting the fire that engulfed the oak tree. We always blamed him for everything.

We learned a lesson that day: When in trouble, go on the offensive. Rather than admit that we were the culprits, we pretended to be heroes, alerting everyone there of the danger. I responded the same way when, in my late 20s, I had a part-time job at the Press Democrat Newspaper in Santa Rosa, which required that I be on the loading dock at midnight. One night when I was drunk and overslept, someone else was called to take my job for the night. Monday morning, I stormed into the circulation manager's office, saying, "Charlie, we need to talk!" I have no idea what I said next, but he was caught off balance and I got off with a mild admonition not to be a no-show again.

From childhood into my 20s, angry feelings about authority seemed to haunt me. Once I walked out of a science class in junior college because I was disgusted with the teacher. On the way out, I let him know what I thought of him and his lack of regard for students. Later, the school dean got us both into his office and demanded that I apologize for not showing respect to the teacher. I agreed to do so if he apologized to me for not showing respect to students in his class. The teacher apologized, but where did I get off doing that kind of thing?

It wasn't the only time I bucked authority head-on. When I was working toward a master's degree at San Francisco State College, I thought one of my professors was so inept that I organized a small study group to get through the required statistics class. Few of us seemed to be learning anything in class, and I was determined to learn what I needed so I could use it on my master's thesis. We worked our butts off and actually got a pretty good understanding of the course content. When I received a "B" grade, however, I burst into the professor's office and demanded that he give me an "A" or an "F." I forget exactly what I said but it was something about studying our hearts out and having a decent grasp on the material and that the final test did not represent our learning. I got my "A."

These adult scrapes with authority were part of my tendency to act out without thinking, which often caused problems. As a kid I was kind of mouthy and often stirred up trouble by what I said. I was slight, so my mind was a better defense than my fists. My friend Gilbert was a fighting machine. We stood up for each other. He not only excelled at fighting but also liked it. Once when I was 18 and on leave from the Navy, I visited him and our sidekick in San Francisco. We went out cruising and drove onto a street that was dark and empty of traffic. Our headlights were the only illumination, except for what looked like a naked bulb in the upstairs window of a building. Gilbert was driving, and we, his passengers, were squeezed into the front seat, like teenagers on a date.

In the gloom, we drifted past an equally dark four-door sedan full of guys and girls and made a smart aleck comment to the girls. That's when our problems began. Bam! The other car lunged backward, some heated words were exchanged and the boys got out of both cars. Gilbert kept a bicycle chain on the floorboards for occasions like this, and he came out the door of the coupe swinging. Kids scattered. He was cleaning house. At one point I picked up an empty quart beer bottle to smash against someone's head and the chain whipped my direction, breaking the bottle in two. The next swing left a vicious gash in my forehead.

"Get in the car!" We piled in, our sidekick, Jack, behind the wheel, with Gilbert jumping on the running board as we sped away. He told us later he didn't need the chain after awhile and had dropped it to just use his fists. Someone from the other car had picked it up and was wailing away at us. We floor-boarded it out of there and on to brighter streets to safety. Blood was pouring from my head wound, I could smell it, but we were riding with adrenaline at a fever pitch and grooved on into the night.

I didn't know it that night but Gilbert was acquiring a heroin habit. He told me about it later and described his routine for obtaining and using the drug. He would go to an apartment in Chinatown in San Francisco to pick up a package of H. This was in the days when heroin was a heavy- duty street drug so Gilbert kept a coded phone number in his wallet. To decipher one had to subtract each number from 10. So if the number 4 appeared in the coded number, the actual number to dial would be 6. He would park near an apartment, go inside, pay a man and come out with a packet of the white powder. He then drove to an entirely different part of town where he had stashed a kit for injecting the drug. In a dingy public toilet on the 7$^{th}$ floor, he recovered a spoon, a needle and a rubber strap from the top of the stanchion. This was his routine – heat the heroin in a spoon, clear the needle of air bubbles, draw the liquid into the needle, then with the strap wrapped around his forearm, insert the drug into a vein sending it directly to the bloodstream. He experienced instant euphoria and in a larger sense, loss of life as he had known it. Gilbert was never the same after this drug took over his life.

Just as these events had happened outside the home, my greatest adventures at Lytton were on the road, running away from it.

# CHAPTER 7

## *Running Away*

Being on the run was exciting. Running away became a pattern for me, and I can remember the first time I did it, after being in the home only a few months. I walked up the county road and hid in the bushes whenever a car approached. The county road meandered past empty fields and an occasional vineyard. It had no shoulders; instead, grassy ditches lined the dark asphalt. Drivers had to rely on their skill rounding corners for there was no centerline. This was the dumbest runaway trip ever, and there must have been six or eight of us making it. I was one of smallest and a tag-along. Big Ted picked us up in the home's green carryall within the first hour. He gave us a stern lecture and took us back to the home.

I had a more successful trip about a year later one warm October day when four of us set out, heading east toward Highway 128. I was 11 at the time. This was the same highway that branched from Cloverdale to Booneville and the coast. A rural two-lane road, it moved east up Alexander Valley and into Napa County. We were a grungy group, four skinny white kids with untamed hair flopping over our foreheads. Almost like uniforms, we each wore white T-shirts and very dirty Levis. A pack of Camel cigarettes was lodged in my Levi pocket. I had on sneakers, and the three others wore street shoes.

From the Lytton gate we walked the three miles past prune orchards to the Russian River, where a small grocery store sits by the bridge. We were tired by this time—no one had given us a ride—and wondering whether our decision to take this road had been a good one. We were getting hungry but we had no money for the store. We continued to walk, forking to the right over the bridge. Sweating as we trudged, now on Alexander Valley Road, we found our pace was getting slower and our spirits falling. How could we get food? Where would we be at nightfall? What could we do for shelter? We carefully watched the farmhouses we passed, worried that someone might see us and think we were enough out of place in this setting to call the cops. On our right were desolate vineyards, fields lined with the gnarled remains of a summer grape crop. Close to the paved road stood a faded wood barn, with a sign proclaiming it a winery, with a tractor and a pick-up truck parked in the yard.

Passing the winery, we spotted a farmhouse. It was set far enough back from the road that it appeared isolated, maybe a good place for a break-in. We figured that we could grab some food, and if cash were lying around, or cigarettes, so much the better. The gravel driveway was empty, the faded yellow curtains in the house windows were closed and there was no sign of life, so we began to approach the house, trying to appear natural. If someone was home, we would say we were looking for a drink of water. We were in the front yard and climbing onto the porch when we heard a ruckus up the hill. A school sat perched on a knoll about 200 yards away. There were swings and tetherball poles in the yard, but no one was playing there. Instead, children were at the end of the playground closest to us, yelling and pointing in our direction. All of a sudden they started running toward us, as if to protect the property on which we were trespassing, and the school bell began to peal.

Frozen on the porch, I felt my mouth go dry and heart ratchet up a zillion beats. We had only one option: run. We bolted from the farm property, heading diagonally for a hill away from the kids. The mob swerved and went that way too, as if to head us off. We pushed on harder, running for our lives, with lungs bursting and legs seeming not able to pump any more. Still we ran, up into the open hills. The kids were behind us now. We had gained a little distance from them, but now they were hitting the slope of the hill fresher than we were and we didn't know if we could run anymore.

With no other options, we had to keep going. Gasping, staggering forward, we would only pause to catch our breath and then push forward some more. Ahead we could see where the landscape changed from open grass to intermittent Manzanita and oak trees. If we reached the trees, we could be safe.

When we found we absolutely could not run anymore, we looked back. The kids had stopped chasing us, apparently called back by their teacher. Dropping to the ground, we caught our breath and then talked excitedly about our narrow escape, laughing and congratulating ourselves for fast thinking and fast feet. We stayed in the hills awhile and did not return to the road until it made a sharp turn to the left, miles from and clearly out of sight of the school kids who had been chasing us.

## HIDING IN PLAIN SIGHT

On another occasion, I was involved in a run-away even though I never left the home. This time I was an accomplice, not the "escapee." JT was my age. He ran away and hid in the attic over the school, in the part of the building where there was an assembly room that was used for Sunday church services. He was a reasonably bright kid, but I have no idea what he was thinking. He stayed hidden in the musty attic for six days while the deans fretted and waited for news of his recovery from the police in some nearby town. Meanwhile, a few of us sneaked food out of the dining room on a regular basis and brought it to him. He had fun moving about different parts of the attic, listening to people below. I imagine, though, that he must have been lonely there. He was finally caught when, ceasing to be careful as he moved too fast across the beams, his foot came crashing through the ceiling in the assembly room. JT was later adopted out of the home, the only kid I knew for whom this to be the case. He was 15 and was adopted by a mortician; later he entered the profession with his dad. His twin, JL, was last seen on skid row in Modesto, California.

Several of us found adventure in a different attic, one above the small art and crafts building near the gymnasium. We went there to play poker. I don't know if playing poker was illegal, probably not, but where and how we played it was certainly not the usual way. Red and blue poker chips and two decks of cards were kept there, where we had dragged an old card table and fashioned makeshift seats. In the center of the card table lay a BB pistol. The goal of the game was to cheat and not get caught. A player suspecting a cheater would move for the pistol to shoot the offender, and of course the kid who was going to be shot also lunged for it. BBs were fired by the quicker "draw." It's a wonder one of us didn't lose an eye. When we were outside, in the spirit of good westerns, we would lean indolently against a wall and with a sneer on our lips slowly bring a lighted cigarette into our hand embers first to crush it out. To show pain was not allowed.

## GUN IN MY FACE

"Get the hell out of there," the man shouted. "Right now!" He pushed a handgun right between the noses of me and JT. All was quiet at 2:00 am; the streets were empty, even the main drag of Gilroy, the southernmost city in Santa Clara County in the San Francisco Bay area. We had gotten there about a half hour earlier, heading downtown along The 101.

The night before, JT and I had slept in a horse barn in Palo Alto. That night it was rainy and cold, the kind of cold that goes right through to your bones. We were both skinny kids and freezing, so when we saw a barn on a huge tract of land being developed for houses near the bay, my buddy had the idea of lying on the horse in the barn to absorb their body heat. It worked, warming me, but I couldn't sleep much lying on the back of the huge animal.

Earlier that day we had walked through South San Francisco. Being hungry, we had tried to snatch a couple of bananas off a bunch hanging outside a grocery store. The whole bunch dropped into my arms, and we did our best to be inconspicuous carrying it through the city and onto the highway, leaving town.

On this run-away from Lytton, we had scraped up a few cents so we could ride on a Greyhound bus. It stopped in Gilroy to let us off, and we were scouting for a place to sleep when we ambled toward a Chevron station to get a drink of water. The station was closed, as was everything around it, being the middle of the night. This was when we first saw the dark car, gliding slowly in our direction as in a dream. Three men were inside as the coupe silently entered the gas station property. We didn't know what to make of this and "strolled" to the other side, away from it, but the car followed. Alarmed now, we ran—down a street, then an alley, and even jumped a fence higher than I thought was possible. On the other side, we hid for what seemed an hour. The car must be gone, we thought as we cautiously left our hiding place. But then we spotted it, and the car sped toward us again. Panicked now, we ran across the main drag and hid underneath one of the out-of-service Greyhound buses parked there, thinking that we were safe.

Then we saw the gun in the hand of one of the three men who had been following us. I was scared shitless. JT compliantly inched his way toward the man holding the gun as I inched backward, toward the opposite side of the bus. I got to my feet and ran screaming down the middle of The 101, the big man chasing me down the empty highway. "Help! Help! Somebody help!" I yelled, screaming my throat raw. "I didn't do anything. Leave me alone. Help! Help! Somebody help!" I repeated at the top of my lungs as I ran, terrified, knowing I was going to die.

I had no chance of escaping the long legs of the man chasing me. After he caught me, he dragged me and my friend back to where the other men were. "Get in the car." We were jammed into the car with them. My mind spun wildly. Who were they? Had we stumbled upon a mob operation? Or were these college men out for a good time and trying to scare us? Both of us were silent in that cramped vehicle as they drove away quietly, down the main street of the town, and then turned. Hallelujah! They were taking us to a police station. That night, the police were my best friends in the universe.

The three men turned out to be off-duty cops. They had taken us for gang kids out looking for trouble. We ended up spending a few nights in the local jail before being transported back to Lytton.

## SAN RAFAEL

Not long after the Gilroy episode, the cops picked Gilbert and me up, this time in San Rafael. We were heading for San Francisco when they got us for hitchhiking on the highway. So the Gilroy jail one night and a few months later the San Rafael Detention Center. Life was looking up.

Gilbert and I would have died for each other. He was as adventurous as I was and confided in me things he had never told anyone. His parents were Christian Scientists, like mine, so we could relate about some family things. He was moody and could not, or would not, relate to adults. He was one of the kids lost to life, becoming addicted to heroin before he was 18, but as kids we were inseparable.

On this occasion we were hitchhiking south toward San Francisco, and then the police cut our trip short, taking us instead to San Rafael. We were interviewed and then sat in the police station waiting, and then waiting some more. When it became apparent that no one was really paying attention to us, with a look and a nod to each other we edged closer to the door, feigning interest in the wanted posters and other announcements on the walls. Then we broke from the station, Gilbert running off in one direction and I toward another.

I slept that night behind a billboard on ground covered with ants. "Slept" might not be the right word, as I look back on it. Shivering, slapping at ants, scratching myself, moving my body this way and that to escape them, I would drift off only to be awakened time and again by their relentless activity. The cops picked me up the next morning as I headed for the highway to hitch hike. They had caught Gilbert the previous night at the bus station, where he was trying to sneak aboard a Greyhound. We both got to spend a few days at the San Rafael juvenile home before being sent back to Lytton. It was at the juvie, however, that I was introduced to a new fruit–honey melon. I got to eat some in what I remember as being a pleasant place for a juvie, sunny with lots of windows.

## TO SAN DIEGO

On another occasion, a boy, whose most distinguishing feature was crooked green teeth, and I were hitchhiking. We first made it as far as the central valley of California, sleeping in odd places a couple of nights along the way. Gabriel was younger than I, a follower, not a peer, but together we made it all the way to San Diego.

Farm equipment, long-distance carriers and passenger cars populated the four-lane highway out of Salinas, along which we had been standing for almost an hour, temporarily discouraged as we extended our thumbs to stop an approaching vehicle. A pick-up truck filled with Mexican farm workers stopped, and the driver said he could take us as far as Soledad if we could hang out with them a little while as they took a detour to a nearby town to the east of the highway. It sounded good to us, so we rode to Chualar, bouncing in the back of the truck with the smells of fresh earth and cow manure in our noses. Chualar mostly had a few bars, and the group, including the driver, disappeared into the one closest to us. As Chualar was largely Hispanic, we knew we white boys stood out, so we waited in the back of that old pickup for the men to return. We waited and waited, getting anxious. We had no idea where we were, or where The 101 was, so how could we get out of there? After what seemed an eternity, the men returned, rolling with drink, and proceeded to Soledad. It was one of the longest rides of my life, in an ancient vehicle that swerved from side to side on the country road while the men sang their hearts out.

Back on The 101, my friend and I hitched to King City, a bend in the road, after miles of pretty much nothing. South of the town were San Lucas, Bradley, San Miguel, San Ardo and Paso Robles, but they were hours away over desolate territory, and it was hard to hitch anything but short rides. The 101 virtually entered this farming town with one trajectory and then exited at a different angle. The town was small—as late as 2000, its population was 11,000—and to our eyes the 2.8 square miles of the city seemed uninspiring like the area around it, even if it did boast that an early settler was the father of John Steinbeck.

We stood, thumbs extended in proper hitchhiking form on the southern end of town. We stood. We paced. We stamped our feet and stood some more. We smoked cigarettes to help pass the time. Minutes passed. Hours. There was very little traffic on this stretch of the highway and few were willing to pick up grungy-looking kids who looked like they might have slept outside for a few nights. Maybe we could board a bus at twilight for, say, San Miguel and hope the driver would forget we were on it and keep on going. But to board a bus, we needed money, so we hatched a plan.

Near the south end of town was a liquor store, a stand-alone building nestled between several others whose windows had flashing beer signs, cigarette ads and pin-ups advertising beer on them. In front were three newspaper racks—for the Fresno Bee, San Francisco Chronicle and a local paper. In the back of the store were stacks of empty coke bottles, beer bottles and other soft drink containers. Stacked in cases, they made for easy carrying.

After quietly lifting two cases of empty cokes, we carried them around the side of the building and inside through the front door. Hardly looking at us, the man behind the counter refunded "our" money, and so, at twilight, we boarded a bus for Bradley, which was as far as our money would take us. There the driver made a routine stop, letting on a couple of passengers. At the back of the bus, we feigned sleep, and as the bus pulled back onto the highway we breathed a huge sigh of relief. So for 35 or 50 cents or so, we each got a ride from King City to Los Angeles, a distance of over 200 miles.

The Greyhound station in Los Angeles was a zoo, with dozens of buses poised to depart, passengers milling everywhere, disembodied loudspeakers announcing departures, destinations emblazoned on signs on the front of vehicles. A bus for San Diego was parked in a middle lane, far away from the eyes of officials and ticket-takers, so we picked that one to board, went to the back and once again feigned sleep. Undetected, our few pennies from the Coke bottle returns took us all the way to the southern tip of the state, more than 500 miles from our starting place at Lytton.

I stayed in San Diego for a month, ditching my companion a few days after arriving there. To get some money, we snatched newspapers from storefronts before the stores were open and then sold them on the street. I even swiped papers from doorsteps of homes. On an earlier run away trip to San Francisco, I took one off a porch at the same time a man came out of the house to get his paper. I was on a bike and still he chased me, up one of the city's steep hills, and I pumped my heart out to get away.

Our San Diego plan, which usually worked, was to pick up bundles of papers at stores then hawk individual copies on the street. One day a newsvendor saw us selling papers and asked us to cross the intersection to talk to him. What we learned was that newspapers companies, including the San Diego Tribune, marked the front page of each paper indicating its sales venue: store, street, or home. We were caught. The vendor asked us to wait while he went across the street to talk to a cop in a police cruiser, so of course we ran.

Heading down an alley, I got ahead of Gabriel and beyond his sight. I scrambled behind a large sign and hid there, where I could see my friend huffing down the alley, with the newsvendor running and puffing behind him. I could sense the game. The cop had driven to the end of the alley, and they were running right toward him. As soon as they passed me, I darted out from behind the sign and ran the opposite way. As I broke clear onto the street, I hopped aboard a passing streetcar, letting it take me all the way downtown.

I was on my own now. One way I had of getting money was stealing tips off restaurant counters. I got caught once by a waitress who asked for the dime her father usually left for her. Embarrassed, I slunk out.

I got some new clothes by taking items into dressing rooms in department stores, putting them on over what I was wearing, and then casually walking out. There was no way to take a showers or a bath, so I washed my face and combed my hair at gas stations. I either slept on rooftops, where I felt the safest, or in lumberyards, where I rearranged some wood to make a little cave into which I could crawl and tuck myself in. In San Diego or similar climates, flat-level roofs are often common and easy to reach by climbing a fence. Out of the way of prying eyes, I felt safe sleeping on them. The only problem I remember was waking one up morning to find that a light rain had fallen during the night and I had been sleeping with part of my body in a puddle.

I collected a group of admirers on this trip. School kids discovered my hideout in one of the eastern San Diego canyons, which had sagebrush and scraggly trees. After school we would hang out there, and I would tell stories of my adventures. They would bring me cigarettes. I never wanted for food, because I was good at procuring it for myself. I knew how to shoplift, and the coke bottle scam, filching waitress tips and selling newspapers I stole got me enough money to buy what

I needed. One item I liked to shoplift was a small can of beans with weenies in them made by Dan Campos. I liked the pork and bean flavor of the contents, and the can, being small, was easy to steal and hide. Besides, it had a pull-top lid, which meant it was easy to open.

I used some of the money to go to the movies. This turned out to be my downfall, putting me in the hands of the police more effectively than the corner news-vendor and cop in the patrol car could. "Showboat" was my favorite, and it may have been the only movie I saw because I fell in love with the sad story, the songs, and especially the star, Kathryn Grayson. With Howard Keel, Ava Gardner, Joey Brown and the Champions, a song-and-dance team, it was one hell of a show. I saw it several times at a downtown location, and then one day, as I was leaving the theater, a cop who wanted to know why I wasn't in school stopped me.

"Our house is quarantined. My sister has the measles," I said.

"So you're supposed to be home. Whatcha' doing here?" he replied.

"I'm very sorry. I was just going crazy sitting at home. Nothin' to do. My mom said it was OK," I told him.

He decided to take me home. "Where do you live?" he wanted to know.

"3218 Marlborough Street," I said.

"So where's that?"

"Off University Avenue in East San Diego."

I fidgeted in the squad car as he drove, giving my best impression of a boy who desperately has to go to the bathroom. "Couldn't we stop at a gas station on the way," I asked.

"You can go to the bathroom when we get you home".

The Marlborough house was a 1930s-era construction with a large porch and a front door bordered by two large windows. A paved walkway separated the dry lawn as it sloped down to the sidewalk. When we got to the house, I saw that a building had been erected in the back yard and headed for that, anything to buy time. Attempting to open the gate, I pushed when I should have pulled, and the cop, coming up behind me, commented about that. He asked a woman who was there if she knew "this boy."

"Absolutely not," she said. Well now the cop was annoyed. I told him I hadn't given him my real address because I would get in trouble at home, but he wasn't buying it. I then gave him another addresses—my "real one" this time, on Morningside Way in La Mesa, even farther east. This house sat on a hill, with terraced gardens below it. My plan was that when a woman opened the door I would push past her and run out the back door and into the back yard, making my escape. It was not to be. The woman stood behind the screen door to talk to us.

Back in the squad car, I had run out of stories. I finally told the cop I had run away from a children's home in Northern California and the rest of it. Disgruntled, he drove me back to the downtown precinct station, and by the time we arrived there, he was in a better mood, singing, *"San Francisco, here we come"* to the sergeant.

## JUVIE HALL

From there I was sent to the San Diego Juvenile Detention Center in Mission Valley, which was then named Anthony Home. I was there for two weeks until transportation could be arranged to take me back to Lytton.

Even today I have an emotional, visceral reaction when seeing prison films. I know what it felt like to be a prisoner. At the detention center we wore identical denims—pants, shirts, and jackets. Unlike in the movies, where you see two prisoners to a cell, our bunk beds were in a dorm-like setting, each with a wafer-thin mattress and a layer of woven metal as the springs. I remember waking in the top bunk one night as two older boys pulled down my shorts and were fondling my butt. I scared them off by yelling, but I was scared. They didn't bother me again. Smokes were hard to get so we rolled pencil shavings into cigarette paper, and when we lit up it was like putting our lungs on fire.

I witnessed fights in the exercise yard. One day a Mexican kid of middle height, sturdily built with tattoos on his arms and face and dark beard stubble on his face, slouched slowly up to an adversary. Arms extended, palms up, and with a smile on his face, he said, "Hey, we're cool, man." Before the friendly tone of his voice faded, with rattlesnake quickness he struck the face of the other kid. When the kid fell, the Mexican kicked him repeatedly in the ribs and head. There were mostly street toughened Mexican and black kids there when I was being held, and I was often frightened just being around them.

By the time I was returned to Lytton, the season had changed. Green grass announced that it was fall in Northern California. I was down to skin and bones but had no idea I had lost weight until I tried to wear my former clothes. Two women had driven me back to the facility with a 14-year-old girl who was being delivered to Los Guilicos, a girls' detention center for the Sonoma County Juvenile Justice Center, near Sonoma. I rarely pass that spot today without thinking of the ride from San Diego with her. Our keepers were probably social workers, though they acted more like the probation workers I later worked with as an adult. One of them would turn from time to time and shine the flashlight into the back seat on her two charges to make sure that we were not doing any hanky-panky. We were both offended by the suspicion and flashlight treatment, and whispering in the back seat, we planned an escape. A stop in any town, we reasoned, would be an opportunity for us to get out of the car, stretch our legs, and then make a break for it. We would steal a car and then … . I think that's as far as we got in planning to escape. The opportunity to do so never arose.

## WE GIVE UP

On another occasion I went north into Oregon with Eugene Bishop. It was bitter cold, with snow flurries in the air. We slept in sawmill yards, on the cold cement floor in a gas station, hotel lobbies until kicked out, and in the back of a station wagon parked in a used car lot. In the men's room at gas stations, we stuffed newspapers under the door in an effort to keep out the frigid air. Nothing worked. We shivered until our bodies hurt. We had to move frequently during the night, either chased off or because we couldn't get warm where we were. My companion knew something about lumber operations so he guided us to a huge smoking cone in a sawmill known as a wigwam. This one looked like that, a giant wigwam, standing several stories into the air, with smoke and sparks coming out from the top. Wastes from the mill were burned there. There were tunnels at ground level, and inside them the roar was deafening as the ignited sawdust and other wastes soared and sounded in the air. We went inside the one with the least amount of ash, meaning a volcanic-shaped pile less than 8 feet tall sat on the dirt floor. The ash mounds were taller in other tunnels, however, nearly blocking the sight lines beyond them. Some tunnels were even filled with the hot ash. Inside our tunnel we could look up into the center of the cone and see the space above us filled with burning embers, fluttering this way and that, up and down, on drafts of air. Our tunnel had enough room for us to sit against the wall in the wonderful warmth of the fire. If we stayed too long, especially if we fell asleep, we would likely become a part of the fire.

Although we were finally warm, we spent a truly miserable night afraid to fall asleep, and at dawn we hitched out of town. For the first time on a run-away, we gave up. There was a freezing fog, and at a highway intersection a work crew in yellow slickers struggled with repairs on the fork we were not to take. Headlights appeared in the fog and passed us, probably because drivers were not able to see us or, if they did, because it was by then too late for them to stop. We stood for hours in a light snowstorm, becoming more and more despondent as fresh deposits drenched our heads and shoulders and we stamped our feet to try to get feeling back. At long last, we flagged down a police car and told the cops our situation. There wasn't any juvie in this small town, so they lodged us in the jail, taking us across the street to a restaurant for meals.

## BACK AT THE HOME

Returning from run-aways was almost as much of an adventure as the trips themselves. The season had changed by the time I returned from the San Diego trip. Other times there was a sense of freshness to the home when I returned. I don't remember what kind of a reception I got from the staff—there seemed to be no special consequences for missing school and I had interesting stories to tell the kids there.

I read a lot of Mark Twain stories in those days, reveling in the trips Tom, Huck and Jim took down the Mississippi; the tricks the boys played on adults and on each other; the sense of absolute freedom, endless days with no responsibilities, and self-sufficiency. I dreamed of being able to raft down a major river someday, not just any river but the mighty Mississippi. With building tree huts, running away, and having other adventures on long summer days, I thought I knew what Tom and Huck must have felt from their experiences.

When I was in about seventh or eighth grade, I started to "publish" a newspaper. Since this was well before any access to photocopiers or ditto machines, the paper's circulation number stayed at one. My paper consisted of two 8-by-11 pages with stories neatly penciled into two columns, headlines and hand-drawn pictures. I probably made two or three editions before abandoning the project, but I remember that it marked my early interest in writing. This was about the same time that I was writing poetry. One poem in particular sticks in my head and seemed prophetic for my life. I wrote it when I was fourteen.

## TRAVELIN'

*Pack up and unpack*

*That's all I seem to do*

*Yet every time I do it*

*I travel somewhere new.*

*I'm not complaining of my lot*

*Yet it can kind of get*

*A little tiresome now and then*

*When I'd just like to set.*

*—RJG*

In a photo of me at age 13, showing me with slicked back hair and wearing pressed pants and a sport coat, I am standing behind a Greyhound bus. Twice a year I traveled by bus for a two-week vacation at my parents' home. Add to this a lot of hitchhiking I did on run-aways and the influence of Edgar Guest, and you might see the context for the poem.

Several adults encouraged my poetry writing, notably Gyda Mallory, a nurse who took a liking to Gilbert and me. What I was writing was less important than the encouragement I received from people who expressed interest. The adult influences in my life during that time turned me toward a totally different direction than the one in which I was headed.

# CHAPTER 8

## *Adults Matter*

For a child, it's the quality, not the quantity, of the time that makes the difference.

### NURSING THE SPIRIT

In my early life, the first adult at Lytton Home who took an interest in me was the nurse I mentioned earlier. She wore her gray hair straight and short and at Lytton was most often seen in a starched white uniform, complete with nurse's cap. She always had a smile on her face for Gilbert and me and became a good friend to both of us.

I felt especially connected to Gyda Mallory, who was from Missouri. When I came to know her she might have been about 50 years of age. It was comforting to have someone to talk to who was interested in me. At the time, I was writing poems. I carefully penciled several in an old bookkeeping ledger and dedicated them to her. She always appreciated hearing a new poem from me. Sometimes I would go up to the hospital and hang out with her. We would talk—I would talk about stuff I was thinking about, that is, and she would give her take on things. She was never shy about her opinions, sharing them unreservedly.

On several occasions she got permission to take three of us into town to eat—Gilbert and me and Jack. On one occasion she hired me to paint the outside of her parents' simple home in Santa Rosa, about 30 minutes south of Lytton. For days, I stood on ladders, brushing paint onto the siding as exacting as I could do, and it felt good to be accomplishing something worthwhile. Being paid for the job was a bonus. I was proud to be asked. This was the first adult labor ever offered to me.

From an old photo, I have a picture in my mind of him sitting hunched into his jacket on the couch in the living room of Sonoma Cottage. His face is sad. His spirit seems somewhere apart from his body. Gilbert was a kid adrift and it was unusual for adults to take an interest in him. Gyda's interest in him was different from his other experiences with adults.

Perhaps Gyda's attention to Gilbert was because the two of us were inseparable, or maybe she got to know him during his long hospital stay after we pulled a dumb stunt together to get out of school. I got a lot of breaks, I think, because I could be emotionally available to adults. Even in school. I can recall getting an "A" in art when I was in the eighth grade while he got a "C." To grade art is crazy to me—it makes no sense, but his ability to draw far exceeded mine.

*Gilbert*

He was a lonely kid. I think I was the only one to ever get close to him, perhaps because, as I said before, we shared a background with parents devoted to Christian Science. We talked about our families and the feelings we had about being at Lytton. He listened to me and even read some of the poems I wrote. If a larger kid ever bothered me, he would get in between us and take the other kid on if necessary. I was like the skinny kid in the "Lean on Me" movie who turned out to be a writer, and he was like the tough buddy who died in the movie. To me, my very best friend was dead before his time, when marijuana and later heroin became the most important things in his life. I grieve for him even today. Once connected to drugs, everything about him seemed to change: his demeanor, his interests, his appearance. He was no longer the friend I knew. A counselor once told me later that he was probably the first love of my life. There was nothing homosexual in our relationship, but we were so committed to each other that we stood as a unit against all odds. Because of this friendship, my expectations in adult friendships have often been too high. I have a vivid memory of our being in a sword fight with sticks. A dozen kids had the two of us backed up behind the cottage, and Gilbert and I stood back to back, fending off their attacks like swashbuckling pirates.

Once in a blue moon a bike shop brought rental bikes out to the home. If a kid had money, he could rent a bike for a few hours. Gilbert and I once rented a tandem bike and nearly killed ourselves trying to navigate turns on it on the county road. In San Francisco, we hitched rides on Coca Cola trucks while riding on our bikes, holding on for dear life and hoping the driver did not stop too suddenly.

Gyda watched over us through all of this, patching us up when we were hurt and letting us know very clearly went she disagreed with what we were doing. After I left Lytton, I continued to be in contact with Gyda. We would see each other once in a while for a meal. I would visit at her house. For a period, she babysat for my two girls while their mother Irene and I worked. Extremely conservative in her religious views, she did not tolerate any swearing around her and freely expressed her devotion to God and to Jesus. She was a very good woman as well as one of the few people at Lytton who took an interest in me.

## BEATING THE SYSTEM

We both met Gyda through a stupid trick Gilbert and I pulled. Actually, with the pain now a distant memory, I think it was quite a creative approach to solving a problem. In order to graduate, eighth-graders in California were required to take a test about the U.S. Constitution. One kid in our class got our respect due to ingenuity, but also our disdain due to his stupidity. He figured that if he couldn't write on the day of the test, he couldn't be tested. Full of resolve, he took a lead pipe and came down hard on his left wrist, as he was left-handed, shattering the bone. It worked—no test for him. He got to wear a big white cast, which all the kids signed. But adults, being the tricky creatures we thought they were, found a way to test him later, orally.

While Gilbert and I had no need to duck the graduation test, we found the idea of getting out of school for a few days appealing. What could we do, though, so we could skip school without there being an argument about it? The lead pipe ploy was out: It had been done before; our wrists were small boned and probably would get crushed if we tried it, and besides, it was just plain stupid.

We found our inspiration to beat the system behind the cottage. Near the county road where we had buried the stolen cigarettes there grew in three-leafed glory some poison oak plants. Would rubbing it on our face, near our eyes, we wondered, cause enough swelling that it would be difficult for us to see? This may have been the start of my relationship with Gyda; in any case, you could say that it blossomed after this episode.

The poison oak worked so well that we were both temporarily blind. With faces swollen like cantaloupes, we were assigned to hospital beds for 10 days. Gyda was in charge of the small Lytton hospital, so we had lots of time to talk. At night, the institution's green narrow hallways were dimly lit, and the smell of disinfectant and other medicinal odors were always in the air. Even though the memory of those odors triggers a negative response whenever I visit a hospital now, I think that somehow those days were wonderful for me. Gyda let me have little hospital socks to put on and then I would slide down the waxed hallways in my white gown to follow her on her rounds.

I had time to think in the hospital. One can only sleep so much, and on nights when Gyda was not on duty I reflected about my life. Why was I unpopular and picked on? Kids stole stuff from my locker and then laughed about it. One of them snubbed me, I was afraid of another, someone didn't like me, and others teased me constantly. I was accused of things I hadn't done. It wasn't my fault—they were jerks—nobody understood, I thought. But gradually, through the miracle of loneliness and the reflection that it prompted, I began thinking about things differently. I imagine myself in that hospital bed seeing my life as a movie. From that perspective, I was able to see some of the effects I had on others.

*Bob at Lytton*

Maybe the problem was me. Maybe I was inviting trouble. I thought about this for a few days, wondering what I could do differently.

I did behave differently after my stay in the hospital visit, and my life improved. My issues with authority continued, however, especially in school.

## TEACHERS

Four teachers occupy my memory from grade school through as much as I finished of high school. When we found out our eighth-grade teacher's name was Gladys, some of us begin referring to her as "happy bottom." In her class, you could hear a pin drop, so I delighted in annoying her by making noises with my pencil as I was working on a paper of problems in fractions. Because they were all simple calculations, I could do them at breakneck speed, and did, drawing scowls from her. I was doing my work, though, so she could do nothing about it.

I had a teacher for two years, in sixth and seventh grades, whose way of disciplining was focused on a boy's hair. At the first infraction, Mr. J. would step behind me at my desk, take the patch of hair above my right ear between his thumb and index finger, jerk and pull it at the same time in a rotary fashion. That got my attention. If there were a second offense, he would use both hands, pulling more vigorously above both my ears. This really hurt, and I would move my head and strain my body toward his hands to ease the pain. In response to a third violation, he would slam my forehead onto my desk after pulling my hair, as if to bang some sense into my noggin. If all this failed and I committed another infraction, I was off to the cloakroom, where a strap was waiting. Each year, I had the distinction of being the first kid to be strapped by this teacher.

My time at Healdsburg High School was a calamity, except for when I was in Miss Distrell's class. She taught English literature. Apart from paying attention in her class, I was a walking disaster—first in the school to lose all 100 merits assigned at the beginning of the each quarter (actually, I usually tied with a kid from the town). I was disrespectful, rebellious, and tardy or absent, and I don't remember all the other minor infractions I was charged with. What I do remember is sitting in the principal's office totally numb and uncaring. I could deaden myself to anxiety or any feelings about consequence. I also remember with some relish my seventh-period freshman English class. Our group became such a problem that the school went through six substitutes before the regular teacher returned from illness at the end of the term. When she returned, she grabbed me by the ear and pulled me into a seat at the front, saying, "I've been waiting all day for this class."

The classroom was located on neither the first floor of the building nor the second but somewhere in between as the building was built on a slope. I occupied a seat next to the window, as did a couple of my friends. When the substitute's back was turned, we would drop out the window onto the ground below and head up Powell Street to a candy store a couple of blocks away, where we would drink Cokes, smoke and eat Baby Ruth and Big Hunk candy bars until school was out. We thought it was great fun and didn't care about any consequences. On early spring days, there was nothing that could hold me in school. I often escaped with a friend or two to enjoy the lovely weather way before the seventh- period class began.

I remember learning algebra, earning an "A" the first quarter and an "F" for the next and being kicked out in the third. Why? Because I wanted to know why—at least that was at the base of it. Our teacher's goal was to teach formulas, by having us memorize them. Why they worked the way they did should not concern us, but I really was curious and repeatedly asked for explanations. He drove me crazy by not responding, and I guess I drove him crazy by asking. Given my attitude at the time, it might have been the way I asked that annoyed him. When, as a young man, I became a teacher myself, one of my greatest thrills was seeing him at a math conference at which I was presenting. He could not believe I was on the program.

But Miss Distrell stood out like a tropical island in a desolate sea. She was very small, a trim woman with attractive gray hair, sparkling eyes and an iron hand in the classroom. While she tolerated no fooling around, she breathed life and excitement into the English language. Adolescent boys wouldn't breathe a word sideways or pass a note in her class. We read Dickens' *A Tale of Two Cities,* and to this day I envision the carriages on the country roads and Madame Lafarge with her knitting, and sense the tension and excitement in the shadowy espionage and dramatic events occurring in the two cities. I saw Paris as it existed then and was romantically charmed. We also read Shakespeare's *The Merchant of Venice*, and I became incensed at the injustice done to the Jews and the treatment of Shylock. But most of all, and indelibly, she stroked my interest and love for language.

Though I later became a teacher, I had not been consciously propelled to do so by my experience of Miss Distrell. Rather, she gave me a greater gift, one I could enjoy immediately and forever. From her, I gained an appreciation for the wonderful ways words touch and can elevate the human spirit.

## A SOCIAL WORKER FINDS ME

Some relationships last forever. My wife, for example, still sees friends from her college days and keeps in touch with some distant relatives. My relationship with Marabel Beck was one of the few sustaining ones I've had in my life. I met her when I was 12, and for the next 62 years she was a presence in my life. My girls, current wife and I were with her just before she died in March 2007. Even after her death, I've been struck with new realizations about how she looked out for me.

Marabel Beck was a short woman with dark hair and a full face. In a picture I am looking at as I write this she is wearing oversized glasses. Her appearance seemed never to change up until her death at age 94. At Lytton, she had a caseload of 130 kids. I don't know how that compares to normal caseloads but imagine it must have been overwhelming, given some of the difficult kids she worked with, the constant interactions with different agencies, and in some cases dysfunctional and even hostile parents.

The social worker's office was located on one side of the big house where the administrative offices, laundry, dining hall and girls' dormitories were. Her door faced the inner court graveled area. To get a sense of who she was, it is useful to know her mentor. Fritz Redl was a pioneer in residential treatment for troubled children. He was a specialist in psychoeducational interventions. Austrian by birth, he studied with Ana Freud in Vienna and co-founded a residential home in Detroit for boys aged 8 to 12 with behavior problems. He advocated giving love and showing affection with no strings attached. He was a proponent of providing children with gratifying life situations irrespective of their deservedness.

He and his work were great influences on Marabel's approach to her wards at Lytton. She and Fritz became friends and corresponded with one another through the 1950s.

## SANE SEX

One story Marabel related to me in later life tells a bit about her. She had attended the University of Michigan School of Social Work during the Depression. In her junior and senior years, she and six other girls lived on the top floor of a boarding house. Preparing for graduation, they wanted to be informed about life after college, including marriage, and came across a 1919 book entitled *Sane Sex Life and Sane Sex Living*. Since none of them could afford the 25 cents the book cost, they pooled their money to get a copy and then passed it around for everyone to read. Other girls heard about the book, so after Marabel's group was finished, they rented it out. This group of girls, bound together by their college experiences during the Depression, kept in contact for the rest of their lives.

I can remember feeling at age 12 that Marabel liked me. This was so important for a boy like me who had been sent away from home at the age of 7; a boy rejected by his parents—parents who, I learned much later, had even tried to reverse the adoption after it was completed.

Later in her life, I asked her why she took interest in me. She said that I was different from other kids. "In what way?" I asked. "You paid attention to your appearance," she said. "You read literature. Oh, how you read." Also, she added, "The deans were afraid of you." I never did find out why.

She had high expectations for me. She talked about what I was going to do after high school. This fell on deaf ears at least in the short term, as I knew there were no resources for me to go to college. She promoted Reed College, a small liberal arts college in Portland, Oregon where my daughter Wendy now lives. I remember feeling proud but dismissive of her comments. That she could envision me attending college was exhilarating, yet I knew no resources or support would ever come from my parents. I remember feeling the same way when I was finishing my master's degree and a group of professors suggested that I go to Harvard for a doctorate. Given my circumstances at the time, the prospect was laughable.

Marabel and I talked many times in her small office. She was interested in what I had to say and challenged my thinking, asking provocative questions. She was also interesting herself. She liked me even when I caused problems, and when I got into trouble, I knew Marabel would talk to me about it without judging me and would help me consider alternative choices. She listened to my anger about my parents and absorbed the loneliness I felt. She helped me process disappointments, especially in regard to broken promises from my parents. I felt that she respected my intelligence and spoke to me as a person, not as a child.

Marabel went to bat for me at the high school when I was expelled, fighting to get me reinstated. When I refused to go back to school, she negotiated my being placed during the day at her husband's dairy farm, adjoining the home. She arranged for a foster family to take me after it began to be obvious I was not going to survive any longer at Lytton without getting into deeper trouble.

King and Alice Hart, friends of Bob and Marabel from school days in Michigan, agreed to take me into their home with their son, Larry, two years my junior, and Betty their daughter, four years younger than me. The Harts lived in Leucadia, a coastal town 30 miles north of San Diego. It was an ideal placement, even though I was anything but well behaved and caused King and Alice so much angst that after six months they gave up on the prospect of my staying with them through high school. Just before this fateful decision, Marabel wrote me the following letter, excerpted here.

*Mr. Bob Garmston* *December 5, 1950*
*Box 286 Leucadia, California*

*Dear Bob:*

*. . .No one can be of any assistance to another person in any kind of problem, from as simple a one as staying out late to the extreme one of alcoholism, unless that person wants to utilize the "helper's" services. (Incidentally the same holds true in education— no one can successfully teach a person who doesn't want to learn.) The term "helper" probably isn't a wise selection, for in reality people eventually have to settle their own problems, but each of us, in some fashion or other, utilize others' help in trying to come to a better understanding of ourselves, our relations to other people, and some of the things we do and like. Sometimes other*

*people can help us in trying to understand why we persist in doing things that tend to keep us in trouble. Maybe "help" comes accidentally from just being surrounded by people who are friendly and understanding and to whom you can talk about your worries.*

*Last spring following your trip to San Diego, I deliberately tried to get you to examine some of your trouble spots— mainly the relationship to your parents and experiences, hoping that by hauling these situations out into the open you wouldn't have to continue to fight some of the things and people that eventually can bring you reasonable happiness. I recognized then that you had a lot of questions and uncertainties around your parentage and your adoption. No doubt now you are doing a lot of thinking about "you" and possibly even justifying some of your insistence upon doing what you want to do on the basis that these unpleasant things have happened to you.*

*In the meantime, I think it well for you to remember that personal problems do have to be settled around "fact" of a situation and not always what we wish the situation to be. Maybe you need to look at the facts of your present situation. Right now you are living in a home where the people are interested in you, interested not because of just feeling sorry for you, which is one of the things you mentioned last year as not wanting but rather because they have liked you. I think the requests they have made of you in terms of hours, compliance with school regulations etc. have not been extreme and are not outside the realm of those required by the majority of parents within a community.*

*Sincerely Yours,*
*(Mrs.) Marabel S. Beck*
Social Worker

Her letter was typical of her continuing interest in me. Throughout my time with the Harts she communicated with Alice, offered suggestions, and gave encouragement. She reported that even though I was probably not expressing it to them, in letters to Marabel I was confessing a strong attraction to King, and he was becoming very much a father figure to me. (Abstracts and copies of correspondence between Marabel, the Harts and my parents are in the appendix.)

My parents, who by then had moved to Massachusetts, wanted me to return home. Mrs. Beck had suggested they increase the monthly stipend they were paying the foster family for my room and board. I think, too, that perhaps John and Eleanore were becoming alarmed at the affection I was feeling for the Hart family.

Marabel stayed in my corner like a guardian angel. She corresponded with me during my four years in the Navy. After I left the Navy, I returned to Sonoma County, and with my girlfriend Irene, later my wife, also a Lytton kid, spent endless time at Marabel's home talking about "our relationship" (Irene's and mine). When I was drinking too much in junior college, she arranged for a therapist friend to see me for regular sessions. When I got married, she attended our wedding. And when our two daughters were born, she took the same interest in them that she had done with me. Later, after I divorced, Marabel continued to maintain a relationship with my daughters, my ex-wife and me. She and Irene maintained a relationship until Marabel's death.

And every year for my birthday, Marabel sent me a card with a dollar for each year of my life. When I reached 60, she said I was getting too expensive.

I was not the only boy to benefit from Marabel's care. She was a lifeline for two other Lytton boys, Gabby Moore and Duncan McCloud. Tragically, both died, Gabby in a car accident in Petaluma, and Duncan from a diving accident at Bodega Bay. I am still in contact with Duncan's daughter, Bonnie, who Marabel also cared for.

Marabel's heart went out to troubled kids. She and her husband Bob took Gabby into Bob's dairy operation when he was still a Lytton kid, as they later did for me. Gabby's brother led a colorful life and was a poor role model, ending up in federal prison, where he wrote letters to the president seeking clemency. References to Gabby's brother Jim appear in the letters in the appendix referring to Jim's visit to the Harts while I was with them. He sponged off them and contributed to my problem behaviors.

Duncan and I used to chug beer together at a bar in Mark West Springs and ride around wildly in his red MG. I spent war bond money I cashed without telling my wife, and he spent his mustering-out money from the Army. He was a good-looking kid, kind of like a young Sean Connery, with black full eyebrows and a trim, athletic body. His only family was a self-pitying alcoholic mother who lost her life in a San Francisco street car accident and an older brother (whom I met), a longshoreman whose multiple expensive suits hung in his closet, each with a razor blade in the right-hand pocket. He showed us the blades with some pride. Duncan lived a daring life. He was a paratrooper in the Army, a heavy equipment operator in civilian life, and died in a diving accident, with my first wife looking on helplessly from the shore at Bodega Bay.

Marabel was also a lifeline for Duncan's daughter and insinuated herself into the crazy dynamics of her mother's family. Bonnie has the same winning personality as her dad. Bonnie's mother was one of six children, each with a different father, and none of the fathers maintained contact with their kids. Since some of the family members were involved in petty and no-so-petty crime, Duncan's first act was to move his new wife out of that environment.

After he died, Bonnie and her mother went back to that setting. Marabel intervened, not only then but also later, maintaining contact with Bonnie through her teens when she lived with Marabel. I asked her recently what her life might be like today if Marabel had not been in it. "Well," she said, "an uncle wanted me to be tricked out. I was young and pretty, and he figured he could make a fortune off me. Marabel saved me from that."

Without Marabel and the Harts, my foster family to be, my opportunities and aspirations would have remained miniscule. I was kicked out of Healdsburg High School at Lytton and in my junior year dropped out altogether while living in Massachusetts. My biggest goal was to become a sailor. Other kids had joined the Navy or the Army and come back to tell tales. It all sounded more than interesting: unlimited booze, lots of sex, a uniform that announced you were somebody special, and the freedom to make your own choices. Little did I know.

Crediting Marabel for my development would be incomplete without talking about her husband, Bob. He accepted me as a helper on the dairy farm he ran when I had been kicked out of high school at Lytton.

## WORKER MAN

My grandson Ethan was 4 when he began to be fascinated by worker men. By his definition, anyone who came to our house to provide services and wore a tool belt was a worker man. This included electricians, carpenters, gas and electric employees, arborists, plumbers—anyone who had a legitimate reason to wear a heavy belt laden with tools. Ethan would study these men intently, standing to the side, and would adopt "the man way" of standing as he listened to the adults talk. He wanted, he told us, to be a worker man when he grew up.

Bob Beck, Marabel's husband, was a worker man. He didn't wear a tool belt, but he worked with his hands in the operation of the dairy he owned. He leased land adjoining the Lytton property; a swinging gate separated Lytton and the farm. With 35 cows in his milk string, his operation was too small to ever hire someone so he could take a day off. This meant Bob worked 365 days a year, sunrise to sunset, in the rain, the summer heat, the fog, and on holidays. It was true that the only time cows broke through a fence and took to the roads was on a holiday. Bob would need to stop whatever he was doing and run to the area, herd the cows back inside and fix the fence.

When I was expelled from school in April or May of my sophomore year, Marabel arranged to have me work with Bob. I became so fascinated by Bob and working beside him that I refused to return to school, even when Marabel made it possible to go back. I kept on working with Bob until I left Lytton and was placed with the Harts, my foster family.

I loved the work. It was hard, but it was satisfying. I fell in love—I admit it—with cows. I found them lovely creatures, each with a district personality. Later in life, I saw small children in Africa herding livestock and was aware of the immense responsibility they were given. I think this was part of the satisfaction I felt at the farm. I was taught, and then trusted, to do a man's work, caring for and milking the livestock. I remember flopping into bed at night totally exhausted but feeling good about myself.

With Bob, I rode a tractor, cutting and baling hay. I learned about wrapping a gallon water jug with wet burlap so the evaporation would keep the water cool. I mostly watched as he chiseled the blades off the mower in order to replace them, with frequent blows to his knuckles and colorful language. Under his direction I cleaned the milk barn, fed calves, and threw bales of hay in the barn. With Bob, I walked deep into the fields to herd the cows in for milking time. With him, I inspected fences and watched while he repaired breaks. Under his direction I cleared blackberry bushes away from the large barn. This was my first independent project at the dairy, and both Bob and Marabel praised me for the good job I had done.

With Bob, I would wash the udders of the next cow in line and then slip on the milking machine. Under his direction I would poor the milk from the aerator into the large milk cans to be picked up by the milk trucks. With Bob I would drive into Healdsburg for an errand he had to run. We would sit in a tiny coffee shop there, which is where I had my first cup of coffee, laden with cream and sugar and accompanied by a donut. In fact, with Bob I had my first experience of sitting up front in a vehicle with an adult. To ride in the pick-up with him was a thrill in itself. And with Bob I received my first pair of real slacks, purchased at a clothing store in Healdsburg.

He and I would rise at 4 o'clock in the morning, drink our coffee in the house, and then head outdoors for the morning milking and chores. We would return about 9 and eat a huge breakfast and then lie on the floor talking of poetry and life before taking a nap. In mid-afternoon we would head outdoors again for chores, then do the evening milking and cleanup.

Marabel let us know that there was a difference between barn jokes and house jokes. Some, guys' stuff, we could tell when we were out working, while others were fine for mixed company.

Tears come to my eyes as I write about my time at the dairy with Bob. It's almost as if I had not acknowledged to myself the incredible influence he had on my life until now. He died of lung cancer on May 16, 1983. When I went to visit him, I wanted to comfort him, but he seemed resigned to his condition and spent his energy comforting me.

## FOSTER FAMILY

"Tell me another poop joke, Papa." Ethan was 4 and I had just returned from a memorial service for Charles King Hart, the head of my foster family. I was feeling down. "Want to play, Papa?' Ethan asked as he moved toy cars on the floor in my wife's sewing room. I finally relented and began playing cars with him. "Zoom," I would intone as I moved the convertible across the rug. "Beep! Beep! Beep!" one of us would sound as we backed up a huge truck. Finally, with horns sounding and vehicles moving this way and that, we both were laughing.

In the midst of this, Ethan told a poop joke, fashioned as only a 4-year-old can.

"A poop went walking and got hit by a car. Splat!" he said, or something like that.

Before I knew it, we were trading poop jokes. Ethan and I were soon laughing so hard that my wife grabbed a camera to capture the mood. Concerned that this could go on forever unless I found a way to stop it, I said, "No more poop jokes until you're 5." Sure enough, soon after he turned 5, he asked if we could tell some more poop jokes.

The person we had memorialized was a king—his name, in fact, was King—and he taught me, among other things, lessons about aging gracefully. He and his wife, Alice, had lived at White Sands Retirement Home in La Jolla, California, for 20 years, and in the three years before his death I visited them frequently. Alice Hart had died a few years earlier, and characteristic of this man who took reality as it came, upon her death he made efforts to get himself assigned to an assisted living facility, giving up the apartment he and Alice had shared. I'm going to need this before long, he reasoned, so why make two moves when one will do.

Journal entry

13 March 2002

5:45 a.m.

King is gone. March 6 at 10:35 p.m., expiring in a bed on E Floor at White Sands Retirement Home. Everyone was so helpful, so sad, and so attentive in respectful ways, including the young man with the ponytail, a hospice angel, soon after he died.

I understand the meaning of "passed" now as if one literally passes from this body, this world, these relatives, relationships, mental processes—into another world in which the rest of us cannot go. Returning to King's room at 11:00 that evening, I found a cadaver lying in the bed where King once was. An awful stillness, jaw agape and locked, a pale waxed figure of a face with a body shrouded under sheets. There lies the man we called King, so great in life, so empty in death.

Michael, his grandson, and I sat with him until the mortuary man came. Like an apparition

> himself, this huge ebony man entered the room where behind a curtain and in another bed "George" laid, saying "Help" or perhaps asking, as he did through much of his waking hours, "What time is it?" A blessing for King and family that King's mind had not gone off in such a terrible wandering
>
> King is gone. Charles, King Hart, Charlie. Pops to Betty. Silly poppa to Allison. Grandpa to Michael, Ann, Patti and Julie. My father to me. Oh what a wonderful man and such a figure to emulate.

Two things stood out as Michael and I cleaned out his apartment. Three actually. First, how easy it was to dispose of his clothes—not easy emotionally but regarding the choices. Done—everything goes—pants, shoes, ties, coats into huge plastic bags supplied by E Floor staff. Pajamas, too. Like the shell of the man, what gave him physical appearance, set aside without effort. Hats, of course—so Charlie—were saved.

Second, so many photos, and in so many of them King is smiling, exuberant, clowning.

Third, residues of his efforts at being spiritual, being good. Topics he read, notes from many Bible study classes, ways to communicate both personally and in his line of work.

Charles K. Hart, loved by all, never held himself as better than others but simply strived to be better each day than he had the day before.

I am so grateful that I have lived these last eight years with a father, someone I could call "Dad." King called me "Sonnyboy." In these last few years I know I was important to him, and for that I am eternally grateful.

## FROM MICHIGAN TO A FAMILY CONFERENCE

What kind of people had Marabel asked to take me in? The Becks had known King and Alice Hart from Michigan. Alice's mom had died while Alice was in 11th grade. She and her sister lived with her mother's relatives until they were old enough to support themselves.

Alice was an especially determined person, graduating from Northwestern High School in Detroit in 1928, a year after her mom died. She had moved almost every six months throughout her life and was determined to go to just one high school—and did! She had to take two or three trolleys across town to get from where she was living to the school. She attended night schools and worked for the Detroit public schools as a typist, supporting her sister, Marguerite, through college. She had a passion for education and directed it at me.

Charles King Hart had attended the same school, graduating in 1928 as well, but the two never met in the thousand-student high school. He had known Bob Beck in the fifth grade, and then they went to high school together. During the Depression, in the summer of 1930, there were few opportunities for young high school graduates in the Detroit area, and so they went west to Iowa, looking for work. Bob settled into working at a dairy, and King, with chickens. This started a friendly, lifelong rivalry about which was the better animal, a cow or a fowl.

It had been clear to Marabel that I had outlived any benefits that could be had at Lytton and knew I needed to be placed with a foster family. She asked King and Alice, who were living in Southern

California to consider taking me in to live with them until I finished high school. King, Alice, and their children Larry (13) and Betty (10) had a family conference to consider the proposal. Betty had heard bad things about me. She said she was worried that I would kill her chickens. When she was assured that killing animals was not part of my nature, she felt all right about with my joining her family.

## A HOME FOR BOB

The house, on a corner lot, was a former barracks building that had been hauled to Jason Street in Leucadia, California by the previous owners. A lawn and rose garden graced the front of the house. Betty had watering duty there and in the summer would move the hose every five or ten minutes while she read. Both she and Larry were voracious readers.

One entered the mint-green home through the front door, walking directly into the living room. Betty's bedroom was at the front of the house, in the left corner, and the kitchen was to the right, in the other corner. Straight ahead against the far living room wall was a couch the family had brought from Michigan. It had dark upholstery with little flowers, maybe pink or red, and overstuffed arms with a wood armrest in the front that curved up and over. Alice called it a swan couch because of the arms, and she really liked it. Betty, though, thought it smelled dusty and resented having to sleep on it when visitors came. Larry had bunk beds, which Betty coveted, as he never had to yield one to company, but when I came to live with them, I got the top bunk. The kitchen, with its picnic table and benches, was where we gathered—for meals, games and family conversations. If anyone rose from one end of a bench, the person seated at the other end would be upended and dumped.

Betty wrote me some of her recollections recently:

> "You, 15, and Larry, 13, would corral me and sit at one end of the couch emoting the Bard to me. I would sit curled up in the other end, liking both the attention and the writing. I was seldom read aloud to after age 4 because I could read myself! I learned to read at age 4, and in the first grade I read John Steinbeck's *Red Pony*—over Mom's dead body. It came in the Book of the Month Club by default when I was in first grade. This story perplexed me because unlike the stories of the 1940s for

> young kids, this was reality! Dead pony and all and because the boy neglected it. Anyway, so you reading aloud just to me, had a great appeal. Probably your voice had lowered then too—I've always loved the resonance. The only thing I actually remember of what you read was you explaining the words 'Anon!... Anon, my Lord,' so if this is recognizable from one of the plays, we'd know what you read. I always wondered where the Shakespeare book came from. Too highbrow for our family."

She had described for me the house on Jason Street that I recounted above, because I remember very little of it. But I can recall King's saying, "Keep your dirty meat hooks off the woodwork"; or, "Turn off the lights. Who do you think we work for, PG and E?" In some ways, King reminded me of the father in the story *Cheaper by the Dozen* and the man who ran his house like the efficiency expert that King actually was.

I also recall borrowing Larry's bicycle to ride the four miles into Encinitas and the job I got at the Madre Del Oro dairy, where I was able to earn money for incidentals. Later, King bought a lot on Sea Cliff

Drive overlooking the ocean and built a home there. This is where I brought my Navy buddies to come visit with me on weekends.

Unfortunately for the Harts, I was like a spring released from restraints when I went to live with them. I gave King and Alice fits by staying out all hours, coming home drunk, and getting in trouble at school. I was very hard to live with, but even though the Harts didn't know it at the time, I was becoming very fond of them, especially King.

King became the world for me. He would work on projects around the house and listen to me. King was known as a good talker, and he was, but he became an ear into which I could pour my concerns, hopes, fears and stories of daily decisions. If King left the room, I would often follow him, just to be by his side. King was more than a walking encyclopedia, he was an entire set. He knew something useful about everything, not in a pedantic way but because he absorbed information the way some people notice flowers. King was interesting to listen to and could go on at length. He was open to debate, and I had many lively conversations with him. During our talks, it wasn't unusual for one of us to go to the dictionary to define a term or an encyclopedia to check a fact. For me, he was safe. I learned from him, including what it meant to be an honorable and courageous human being. I lived and learned from him for less than a year and then went away, under a cloud because I was causing more trouble than the Harts could manage.

Later when I was serving in the Navy, I spent every weekend I could with King. Alice was important to me, too, but was not the communicator that King was. He treated me as he did his own two kids and talked to me on an adult level. Not only that, he cared about me.

Later in my life, he became an extraordinary model for what it means to age gracefully. His curiosity was insatiable, and he never stopped working to improve himself. He was respected at work and as a deacon in the Presbyterian Church, a good man. I don't think I'll ever reach his stature but know that I am a better person and man from knowing him.

I was 60 when King told me that he and Alice thought that I might turn out OK and wondered if I would like to be adopted by them. Would I! On March 15, 1994, we appeared in juvenile court in San Diego

County for the legal action. The judge was the youngest person in the room. From that day forward I have felt that I have a father. The feeling is like having been ill but not knowing it and now being well. Among the many things I have my wife Sue to be thankful for, this was another. She had suggested to King and Alice that their adopting me would please me.

*Bob and King view map of Bob's Himalayan Trek*

# CHAPTER 9

## *The Navy as Transition*

*Bob in Uniform*

I was 16 when I left the Harts to be with John and Eleanore in Massachusetts. There I was perceived as some form of California freak in the high school culture. I wore pegged pants and had a DA haircut; I slouched and bounced when I walked, like a kid from the Mission District in San Francisco. A perpetual James Dean sneer tortured my lips. I was shy to the point of rudeness. I had no friends. In Springfield, I cut classes, rarely attending school as John and Eleanore thought I was doing. It was cold and snowing. How did these people stand this? I ran away from home. John brought me back.

Tensions in the house were high. John and Eleanore had shouting matches. She accused him of having a German girl friend when he served on the Berlin Air Lift. She complained that he ate steak while the rest of us ate hamburger. She had nothing good to say to him. "Once a sailor, always a sailor" was her constant refrain.

After less than four months of this, I joined the Navy to escape. John and Eleanore were only too glad to sign the permission papers.

The Navy was a reasonable avenue of flight from the icy temperature of life with John and Eleanore and John's "command " posture when telling me what I could and couldn't do. He stood 5 foot 4, but with his nearly 30 years in the Navy commanding men, he was more formidable than any adult I had previously encountered.

"You are not leaving this house wearing those clothes," he said one night, critical of my California-style dirty Levis look.

"What do you mean I'm not wearing these? I bought them. They're my clothes!"

He gave me the commander's stare. "Are you going to take those clothes off, or am I going to take them off you?"

I was intimidated and gave in. He got no more fight out of me.

John's hobbies included fishing and electronics. When I visited in Seattle he took me fishing on Puget Sound. I will always remember the tranquil mornings in the outboard motorboat, with the smells of bait, exhaust and cigarette smoke in the air. In Massachusetts, he let me into his world of radio. In the evenings, I would follow him to the basement. I was quiet around him and would watch him as he typed out Morse code messages at his desk or talked into a microphone with buddies around the globe on his short wave radio. A burning cigarette always sat on the edge of an ashtray overflowing with butts and he always seemed to have a cup of coffee nearby. He had a jar of jellybeans on his workstation and encouraged me to eat my fill of them.

John answered my few questions and would sometimes volunteer what he was doing.

The most personal he got was cautioning me about "camp followers" when he was driving me to the train to go to boot camp. It was a painfully awkward conversation and, in retrospect, caring.

The Navy was a necessary part of my coming of age. I was barely 17 when I entered and almost 21 when I left. The Navy shielded me from being on my own, making decisions about what work to do, where to live, even what to wear every day. At 17, I don't think I was capable of good choices. I was a high school dropout without employable skills, and my attitudes were contrary to getting along in "normal" society. In one sense, the Navy, or at least the bunch of sailors I hung out with, were abnormal in that we were primarily interested in liberty, drink and girls. Our horizons went no further than the next paycheck. And most of us weren't all that successful with girls.

It's said that God takes care of drunks, and I have certainly been protected through some bizarre experiences. While my first experiences with drink were at Oakland and Lytton, I built on these steadily as I got older. Passing out on the highway from drinking Four Roses whiskey, running wild in the Lytton hills with gallon jugs of red wine stolen from the "hermit's" barn are two examples. Later at high school football games in Southern California I knew more about what was going on under the bleachers than what was happening on the field. I met lots of friends at games, none of whom I remembered on school Mondays. After boot camp the Navy was a blur of uninspired duty days, getting off at 16:00 to party and drink, have half-day hangovers, complete the duty day and go out to drink again. It was as if I lived to drink. The Navy culture was permissive and forgiving in that regard. At 17, I was living a dream—a drunk's dream to be sure, but a dream. This was not to say that all was pleasant. I was aware of my life as aimless and unsatisfying.

My education in alcohol progressed at boot camp in Newport, Rhode Island, where I drank most of a fifth of Peppermint Schnapps and got deathly ill. I vomited profusely in a friend's auto. Never again did I drink sweet booze. I was naïve and painfully young. Guys played craps on the barracks floors between rows of bunks. I was smart enough, or scared enough, not to participate as I saw entire paychecks disappear in one or two rolls of the dice. I did bet on college games but rarely won.

After boot camp, I was sent to Jacksonville, Florida, to attend a naval aviation ordinance school. In the 16-week course, I scored 100 percent the first week. The test required memorizing naval abbreviations. I thought this was kind of stupid and from there slid back toward the bottom of the class and ended up graduating last in a group of 216 men.

Drink being available outside the gates, I was drunk most nights and hung over most days. Falling asleep in class earned me the privilege of standing to learn, holding a 20 MM machine gun over my head. I became quite accomplished at this.

I remember particularly a small bar close to the base in which the jukebox played “Hey Good Lookin’” by Hank Williams. The two lines that go ’round in my head are:

*Hey good lookin’ what you got cookin’?*
*How’s about cookin’ something up with me?*

*I’ve got a hopped up Ford and a ten dollar bill*
*I know a spot right over the hill. . .*

I listened to this song over and over and over again. Loneliness lurked beneath the surface, but I rarely gave it voice.

The bar was a small stand-alone building, dark inside with peanut shells and sawdust on the floor. Neon beer signs gave it atmosphere, and two or three couples often weaved drunkenly on the dance floor to the jukebox. There was a pool table at the back, and a game was usually in progress, with a few sailors, beer bottles in hand, lounging around as spectators. The song, the setting and the drink seemed the sad expression of my highest aspirations.

A black sailor and I became good friends, and the two of us went into the bar a couple of times. We also went into Jacksonville on liberty. Against his cautions, we tried to go to a restaurant. This was before the civil rights movement, the sit-ins and the marches in Alabama. At the restaurant a man in bib overalls sitting on the front porch said I could go in the front door and, motioning to the rear, said the other guy has to go in the back. I was stunned. Speechless, I felt nauseous at this ugly realization of racism. After this experience, I took his word that we should not try to go to a movie together.

God does take care of drunks. At least some force seemed to be arranging situations in my favor. I graduated at the bottom of the aviation school class and because the opportunity to choose available billets were based on one's standing in the class, and because most of the guys in my unit were from the east coast, I was able to acquire one of the few billets to San Diego, the county in which the Hart family lived. Nights carousing and inattentive class time made this possible. For the next three years or so, I frequently hitch hiked the short distance from the Navy base to visit them. Our relationship deepened.

Reflecting on this today, I realize that I constructed a home for myself with this family. Nowhere else was home. Not Massachusetts, and certainly not

Lytton. I had no place to go but there. This became a place where I could be the self I desired to be. Here I was the self that enjoyed my "foster" brother Larry and sister Betty. In this place I was liked, even cared for. King, garrulous, playful, a man of clear values, entranced me. He talked with me about topics out of the ordinary. Here I never heard an adult yell. Here was a place that was safe, a place I could talk out my ideas and be taken seriously.

Sometimes on weekends I brought buddies with me to visit. Sister Betty remembers my bringing Ivan, built like a tractor farm boy, and Norman, a Texan intellectual. Norman was the man who 50 years later wrote me to say he was amazed at my accomplishments.

## SAN DIEGO

In San Diego I was assigned to Fighter Squadron Seventy Four within Service Squadron Twelve—in short, FASRON 12. I served time as an aviation ordinance man, a crash crew rescue man, and at the end a journalist, but I arrived as a fuckup, according to the chief petty officer that I reported to. I was fatigued and hung over so he was disgusted with me on first sight. I wasn't too imposing, 135 pounds, a little over 5 foot 9, baby faced and with an attitude. On a last night in Jacksonville, my former post, a lonely lady in a bar picked me up. She had me check us into a hotel for the evening. She was in love, she said, and wanted to marry me. We could slip across the border to Georgia in just a few hours and get married. What did I think?

I'll always remember that night because when we checked into the room the hotel clerk had to quickly extinguish the lights so we wouldn't see the cockroaches scuttling across the bed sheets. Later at the base I learned that such ladies made a living by marrying servicemen in the hopes they would die while serving so they could collect the government insurance for widows.

## HELLO, TEQUILA, IT'S ME, BOB

In San Diego I missed a ship movement—an offense, I was told that could get me shot in a war zone. While I think the officer who told me this was just trying to scare me, it was a serious offense. The squadron was scheduled for a shakedown cruise, and I was stuck in a civilian jail. The cops should have told

Navy authorities they had me but were pissed and vindictive because I had given them such a hard time when they picked me up.

Tequila was a lovely drink. It burned a bit going down and warmed me instantly. There were so many ways to drink it. My favorite was a bite of lime, a lick of salt from my wrist, then a shot bottoms up. I still love the smell of tequila and lime, and this was the way I was drinking it when the cops picked me up.

However, for all its loveliness, Tequila had an unfortunate effect for me. When drunk, I was prone to fight. This is what landed me in a civilian jail and caused me to miss a ship movement. I was drunk in Encinitas, a small town a few miles away from the jail where I was held. The bar was less than half full, only a few others sat at the bar staring at the mirrors and the rows of bottles arranged there. White ones and brown, square ones and round, they all sat there like friends in this lonely town. I don't know who said what to whom, but something set me off. I lunged over the bar in this quiet little town and punched the bartender in the face. When the cops came, they were very clear in their purpose–haul my skinny ass off to jail. I resisted, putting my feet on either side of the doors so they couldn't push me in the paddy wagon. I was the worst kind of drunk.

Missing the ship movement earned me a court marital. I was standing in the hallway waiting for my court appearance when an officer handed me a telegram. *Lt. Commander John Joseph Garmston died on August 25 1952 from a heart attack. Widow advises do not return for funeral.* The blood drained from my face and I felt light headed. I felt alone. I was angry again with Eleanore, who was cutting me off from this most basic of family experiences, grieving the loss of my father. I continued to fume when later she did not bother to call or send me a telegram to reach out to me or acknowledge the loss.

At the court martial I was given 20 days in the brig for missing the ship movement. I emerged from the brig healthier than ever after a regimen of no booze, balanced meals, daily work details, a no-guff relationship to the very serious Marines running the brig, and limited reading material in the cell—a Bible. The brig was the first place ever where I could not fight back. I think missing the ship movement was what also got me drummed out of the fighter squadron and assigned to a crash crew.

## RESCUE MAN ON A CRASH CREW

This was the group of men that was responsible for extinguishing fires and rescuing pilots who crash on carrier decks. I trained for crash crew service at North Island Naval Base in San Diego. On my truck were a driver, two hose men and two rescue men. A big German kid and I were the rescue team, and we got to practice carrying each other up and down ladders in a fireman's carry. I was 135 lbs. and, as luck would have it, he was closer to 180. It was the first and only time in the Navy that I experienced working as a team (my dream before I enlisted), with each person's life dependent on another's action.

My first crash happened during training on North Island. A jet flamed out against the blue sky over the bay, seemed to pause mid-air, and then curled back to crash land near where we were putting out training fires. Training fires were caused by aviation gasoline sloshed onto old fuselages. A torch was thrown into the scene, and we had a fire to practice on. The fire we were rushing to, however, was real. The pilot crash-landed the jet in an open field, the plane skidding finally to a stop. We rode madly to the location and saw him exit the cockpit and run like a banshee away from his aircraft. The thought crossed my mind that we were roaring toward the plane, which could blow up at any moment, while he was running away from it. We noted our relative value to the Navy.

After training, I was assigned to Brown Field as a rescue man on a crash crew. Fate intervened once again, this time to place me in a setting near the greatest drinking culture found near San Diego and in a job that gave me more free time than any other assignment in the Navy.

## BROWN FIELD

Brown Field sits on the Otay Mesa 1.5 miles north of the US/Mexico Border. The elevation is 526 feet. San Ysidro lies on the northern side of the border. On the Mexican side is Tijuana. Previously decommissioned, by 1951 the Navy had reactivated the base due to the increased military activity from the Korean War. Brown Field, when I was there, was isolated from the rest of the naval world; just 80 men manned the facility, including cooks and our "commanding officer," a chief petty officer. Our schedule was 48 hours on duty, 72 hours off, and then the pattern reversed. While on duty, we sat on trucks on the landing field where planes came from North Island and Miramar to practice carrier landings. Sagebrush rolled across the lonely runway on the top of this flat piece of land. At one end the landing strip disappeared in haze bordering the desert. At the other end the hulk of an old plane could be seen embedded in fields of sagebrush. An occasional coyote made its way across the runway.

The pilots using this field would position their mounts over the asphalt strip, drop the wheels, approach, land, gun the engines, take off and circle again for another landing. Our function was to rush to any mishap. When no squadron was actively practicing, we stayed near the barracks, always with boots unlaced and ready to leap to the trucks and jump into our turnouts if required. Helicopters fell from the sky with greater frequency than conventional aircraft. In my time there, four helicopters went down and only one jet crashed.

While on the crash crew, I ran into a Lytton kid. Shorty managed an ambulance that came down from the Naval Hospital in San Diego to sit on the line with us. Strung out on bennies most of the time, he introduced me to this new, for me, way of altering my mind. Benzedrine kept us going; booze took us to a different high. Interestingly, he was one of the kids in whom Marabel had taken interest. I remember she was concerned about Shorty when he was released from the home to live with his brothers in Marin County.

Once when we were conducting a training exercise at Browns Field I realized my romantic notion of Navy teamwork. Like Shadrach, Meshach, and Abednego in the Bible, I stood in the center of a burning inferno yet was not harmed. Here's what happened. As rescue man, I was required to go into the flames, get to the cockpit and execute an extraction of the pilot with my partner. I stood on the wing next to the cockpit. The yellow hot fires engulfed the fuselage and me. I punched the special knife into the dummy's harness, as I was trained to do, and then, with my partner's help, lifted it to my shoulder to carry it out of the raging inferno. As I turned, one of the foam hoses scored a direct hit on my face. The foam mucked the Plexiglas, rendering me blind. I stood, unable to see on the slippery wing of the airplane. Flames still rose around me. After an agony of waiting, a gloved hand reached my gloved hand, and members of my crew formed a human chain. With hands linked to hands, they led me down from the fiery plane. I felt connected, part of a team.

## LIBERTY

Off duty, we would walk the two miles from the base to San Ysidro, or catch a ride if we were lucky. We spent our waking hours in one of three bars, each of which provided the courtesy of a bar bill for servicemen. Beer was 10 cents a glass. Though these were small glasses, it seemed a good price at a time when bread was going for 14 cents a loaf. Beer was the drink of choice for me; though occasionally I would switch to boilermakers–a shot followed by a beer. Another favorite was rum and Coke that I had learned about in Florida. Sweet and with a nice bite, I can still remember the taste in my mind.

My drinking started at 10 or 11 in the morning. Drink and talk, wander to a different bar, drink and talk, wander back to O'Grady's, our favorite. O'Grady's had a good-looking, redheaded bartender, and she was part of the attraction. One night I was too drunk to make it back to base and passed out in a hotel room rented by a fellow sailor. It smelled of feces. I swear I saw some on the bedroom floor. The only furniture I remember was a large bed. I lay down to sleep, covering my body with newspapers in lieu of blankets.

Off the flight line, San Ysidro was our life. Sustenance was mostly the small glasses of 10 cent beer, interspersed occasionally by pickled eggs from a jar on the bar or Portuguese sausage we could purchase from the bartender. Fights, for the most part, happened in the alley outside. I learned a vicious move when a fellow sailor named Clay, a small guy from West Virginia, menacingly approached a man while thrusting his hand in his back pocket as if he had a knife. As the man who had started the fight backed off, Clay kicked him in the balls and he went down immediately. When Clay was on duty and couldn't get out on liberty, he drank after-shave lotion from his locker. I can still see the little green bottles from which he chug-a-lugged—maybe Brut or Mennen Skin Bracer. Most of us never got that bad.

Accidents happened. Sitting in O'Grady's one night I heard a hollow thud, as if a ripe cantaloupe had been thrown on the floor. When my head cleared and I sat up, I realized the sound was from my head hitting the deck. I had tipped backward off my barstool. Such incidents were not that uncommon. After dusting myself off and getting some air in the alley, I was back at my stool drinking.

San Ysidro is one of the world's busiest border crossings, where U.S. Interstate 5 connects to Mexico at Tijuana. Other sailors and I made this journey by car but often by foot, as we could walk from O'Grady's bar into Tijuana, then walk or taxi back. Nothing was off limits there and my naval uniform and young appearance got me numerous calls from the street—"You wanna fock my seester?" I never did, though I have a hazy memory of being led into a huge dark room with sheets dividing spaces arranged for the purpose of quickies with the Tijuana whores.

My worst night in TJ occurred while I was in uniform. I woke in a bar with a terrible taste in my mouth and a tremendous headache. I was in a booth wrapped around a leather seat under the table. My wallet was missing, my white sailor hat on the sticky floor. The stink of cigarettes and booze gave meaning to the dawning sky outside the windows. I had spent the night here. My memory of that night is that I had only two or three drinks. I believe I was slipped a Mickey. Later I was stupid enough to return to the same bar and even worse. I crossed the border one night with a tin of marijuana tucked in my boot. Even at the time I knew this was tremendously stupid! I could have spent the rest of my hitch in a Mexican prison. At that time we smoked pot on the courthouse lawn (at night), in the alleys behind the bars and in the bathrooms, but never, ever took it back to base with us. Pot didn't please me the way alcohol did.

## MOVING OFF BASE AND INTO EDUCATION

In my last year of service, I drank less. Another guy and I decided to live off base. We rented an apartment in a house on D Street in San Diego. A pleasant and generous woman ran the establishment. I remember being invited to Thanksgiving dinner, which we both fully appreciated. The dinner stands out in my mind because she used potato chips to make the dressing. I don't know of anything that ever tasted so good as that succulent turkey that Thursday afternoon. My roommate, Norm, was an interesting guy. Over the top bright and arrogant, he came from a wealthy family. Instead of drinking when he was stressed, he read philosophy. He said it calmed him. The two of us decided to take night classes at San Diego Junior College. I took a literature class and one on Shakespeare. To that date I had never heard poetry read so dramatically. In particular, I remember the teacher's reading E. E. Cummings. Imagine it read with a stage voice, lengthy pauses, special emphasis on certain words, and dramatic volume shifts.

*in Just-*

***spring*** *when the world is* ***mud-***

***luscious*** *the little*

*lame balloonman*

*whistles far and* ***wee***

(This is the way it sounded to me)

During this period Alice Hart encouraged me to take the General Educational Development Test, referred to now as the GED, and apply to my last school district to see if it would grant me a diploma. The school district did. I had unremarkable scores, averaging 20 points below the national percentiles on all but one test. On *Correct Use and Effectiveness of Expression* I scored a 48 to the national percentile of 42. Still barely "average." The diploma didn't mean much to me at the time but I was pleased to have paper from a high school that said I actually existed. Earlier in the Navy, I think out of boredom, I took some correspondence classes. I think they were in writing because I recall getting returned papers marked in red ink.

Looking back, I can see that I had always had an interest in writing; from the newspaper I laboriously produced with penciled drawings, to the poetry I wrote at Lytton, to the journalism class I took at San Dieguito High. I was on the student body newspaper there until I wrote something unflattering (and true) about a teacher. Somehow the journalism teacher let it be printed, which was fine, but I was out. Both Gyda Mallory and Marabel Beck supported my writing interests at Lytton. I don't remember this but was told by Marabel that I used to read to kids in the dormitory. I do remember dedicating an old heavy-bound lined journal to Gyda that was filled with my adolescent poetry. Bob Beck and I, as I mentioned earlier, used to read poems lying on the floor after the morning's milking.

I began to experiment with satisfying personal interests while doing mundane guard duty at night. I memorized Hamlet's soliloquy ("...to be or not to be, that is the question") at night while marching, an MI rifle on my shoulder, from one corner of my post to another. The corners were lighted, so I paused there to check for accuracy. Another accomplishment, of which I am disproportionally proud, was to close my eyes and sleep walk from one corner of the watch to the next.

Our best gig was doing the laundry. This was not principled at all but just plain larceny. At the end of the barracks near the head was a row of washing machines. The cost was 30 cents a load (remember, this was the 1950s). We devised a way of washing for free. The technique was to place a dime at the end of two strips of scotch tape, fix it so the sticky sides were against each other with the dime in between them at the end. With patience, skill and glee, we dunked the dime—once, twice, three times— until the machine growled, cleared its inner mechanisms and began the wash. One dime could serve the entire barracks for months. Now that is economy.

## HONORABLY DISCHARGED

A dip in the national economy brought two changes to my military time. One, the services were told to discharge men a few months early if they intended to enroll in colleges for the fall semester. Two, because of a cash crunch, company commanders got a directive to encourage men to take all their leave before discharge, eliminating the need to pay them off in dollars. I was a squadron journalist at this time, a job that had no operational value at all and a job in which I would surely not be missed if I were off base periodically.

I have no idea how I became the "journalist." Perhaps it was intuitive thinking from higher up that I had proved myself not very capable in fixing bombs beneath planes, clearing and repairing 20 MM canons mounted on wing tips, and that practically anyone could do a crash crew job. I really don't remember how this transition occurred, but I was grateful for it. I was again sent to North Island, this time to learn how to take pictures with a speed graphics camera, the old standby for news photographers.

My specific assignments were to wander around and write human-interest stories that were a credit to the squadron. I turned in about one story a week, banged out on an old Underwood typewriter, got it cleared with Lt. Love, and dispatched it to the base newspaper.

The ruling about leave launched a liberal period in which I appeared before Lt Love, my immediate superior, to frequently request a few days leave in combination with weekends. I trembled standing before his desk, angry with my body for appearing scared, yet was never denied. I used this bonus time to hitchhike the 500 miles to Santa Rosa, where I would eventually go to school and marry.

On 7 September 1954, I was separated from the Navy with an honorable discharge and a final government payment of $214.79 in my pocket. I remember the thrill of walking through the gates in uniform and making my way to the Seven Seas clothing store in downtown San Diego, where I changed from uniform to civvies for the last time. I was also thrilled to have an honorable discharge. I worried about getting less than that my last year in the Navy.

Looking back, I realized the Navy had been good for me in unexpected ways. From my experience on the wing of the burning airplane I learned that men could work as a single unit and function as one in mutual and collective support of one another to achieve a goal. I was to experience this again in small portions during my educational career but most profoundly at Lakewood School, where I was the principal of a school so large and so busy that it felt as if one were living inside a popcorn machine—one explosion in front, then one to the side, then another behind you. All these explosions seemed to require attention simultaneously. I managed this school, cooperatively, with a team—which included a special education teacher, a resource teacher, a community social worker and me as principal. We acted swiftly and coherently and as one. It was intoxicating.

In the Navy I learned I couldn't fight city hall. The institution was too big, too impersonal, too traditionally rule bound for me to push against any portions of it, no matter what I felt or thought. My experience in the brig was the epitome of this understanding in which there was one way, and only one way, to do things. You obeyed or were punished. Push-ups and digging trenches to bury cigarettes and then dig them up again are two examples of senseless punishments. I've watched others fruitlessly expend energy fighting what was not a debatable point. Instead, I've learned to work the system. Much later when I was a principal I got reports in on time even if not important to my operation because central office valued timely reports. This was like learning to wear ties in order to avoid scrutiny in my first teaching assignment. Prompt reporting kept eyes off my operation and me. I'd turn the forms in without delay but use minimum energy, freeing me to use the best of my energy on activities I considered more important.

Principals were to attend district meetings. Sometimes I would not appear, instead meeting with a community group at my school or pursuing another activity that had more value to my central mission than the information I might get at central office meetings. This didn't make me popular but it rendered me effective. Underlying these choices was being my own man, even if inside a larger system than myself.

Unquestionably, the major benefit of my military service was the GI Bill, without which I would never have gone to college. Each month Uncle Sam delivered $110 when I was single and $135 a month after I married. That, supplemented by full-time summer jobs and part-time work when school was in session allowed me to continue my schooling. This was undoubtedly a game changer for my entire life. As a kid I never, ever thought I would attend college.

## COMMUNITY COLLEGE

In September of 1954 I enrolled in Santa Rosa Junior College, rented a room and began taking classes. My housing was located in the back yard of someone's house and had a bed, a wardrobe and a sink. The toilet was in the house. I was totally on my own for the first time. I was 20.

I had lived in institutions for most of the preceding 13 years. My total possessions fit in a footlocker. I was excited, lonely and unsure. I had no parents, no hometown to return to. My one contact was Irene, a former Lytton girl who wrote to me when I was in the Navy. We maintained a periodic correspondence and through letters, I revealed to her the better parts of myself, telling her my activities (censored), my struggles and aspirations. She lived with her sister, also a Lytton kid, in a rented room with private bath, on the street adjoining junior college property.

Without Irene, I may not have survived this post-Navy period. She became in some ways a moral compass for me as she aspired to a normal middle class life having come from intense poverty, deprivation and degradation at the hands of her stepfather. She graduated high school and a secretarial school, had a responsible clerical position at the Exchange Bank, and drove her own car, a 1950 or '52 pale green Studebaker. Those were the "modern" looking cars in which the front looked much like the back.

I was resolved to drink "normally" during this period and remember going to parties with her work group at which I would lecture myself to sip and limit myself to two drinks. I did not know at the time that people with normal relationships with alcohol do not need to work that hard to monitor and limit their drinking. On occasions when we hosted a group in our home, we served martinis. At those events I became word-slurring, falling-down drunk. To me the martini was the very height of sophistication. To drink it straight up with an olive in a martini glass at the top of the Mark in San Francisco was as elegant as I could ever imagine life to be.

*Bob in His Early 20's*

Through the first year of schooling I was wary and shy. I talked with only two people the entire two semesters, both girls. For the first time in my life I studied, taking books home, immersing myself in content, memorizing, underlining. Like most students of that time, I had not been taught how to study, so without clear learning maps, I concentrated and absorbed the best I knew how. I invested in a used Underwood on which to type my papers. Irene corrected my spelling and grammar.

By the end of the year, I had dropped out of school to sell Cutco Cutlery. Door-to-door selling was possibly the worst match for my personality, but the experience taught me how to talk to strangers through memorized sales pitches. Within a few months I was leading men twice my age. Then, with the combination of limited income, continuous rejections, and realizations of how unethical some of our practices were, I quit to go back to school the following year.

What started as correspondence with Irene grew into a romance. We needed each other, though this was not the best foundation for a relationship. During the months before we married, we visited Bob and Marabel often where Bob owned a dairy farm in Alexander Valley. There, inevitably, we would talk with them about our "relationship. Tears fill my eyes as I write this, wishing Irene, too, could visit these memories as I can. She is now housed in a residential home with severe dementia, often not recognizing her own daughters when they come to visit.

On July 31, 1955, Irene and I married in a Methodist church in Encinitas, California, near King and Alice Hart. King and Alice, their kids Larry and Betty, and Bob and Marabel Beck were in attendance. Irene was so excited about the trip that she was unable to sleep the night before the 12-hour drive south. When she began slapping her face to keep awake, we both knew it was time for me to drive the rest of the way.

Irene and I waited almost five years to have children, first Kimberly in 1959, then Judy in 1961. By then I had completed three years of college and started teaching on an internship in Sebastopol, California. This first year of teaching was in lieu of my senior year and paid the handsome rate of three quarters what a beginning teacher would normally earn.

By the time our children were born, I was more than I had been. I was relatively stable, was married, teaching and attending graduate classes. Yet my drinking and arguments with Irene were a constant problem. Most of my development as a responsible grown up was yet to come. Alcohol was to slow the transformation from untamed kid to functioning adult.

# CHAPTER 10

## *Releasing the Grip of Drink*

In my early years of teaching, a lot of the time, I was personally a mess. Professionally I kept the ship afloat, learned a lot, continued to take courses, assumed leadership roles, yet too often after hours and weekends drank to excess. My alcohol consumption gradually increased until one summer in my late 30s when I was drunk or drinking most of the time. One of my friends was a brilliant psychology professor at Sonoma State University. He was also, from the time I first knew him, in advanced stages of alcoholism. A morning at Joe's was always an unknown. Would he be grouchy, sharp tongued and cruel, or would he be happy to see me and consider my presence the greatest gift he could receive? Whichever the case, what was known was that Joe would start the morning drinking after the party the night before. The kitchen counters would be littered with glasses, overflowing ashtrays, plates with unfinished meals, open bottles of vodka, gin or tequila, and paper napkins crumpled across much of the mess. The living room mirrored the kitchen disarray. Later in the morning his wife would rise. The stale smells of food scraps, cigarettes, and booze hovered like a fog over the place. So what was one to do?

Take a drink was the early morning answer. Margaritas, gin fizzes, vodka on the rocks were common choices. If it was dreary and foggy in Joe's Marin County house, mulled wine was the drink of choice.

And most often, once started, the drinking would continue for the rest of the day. Later other people might come by and we could have a party. One weekend I drank non-stop, after which I attempted to drive home from his place in Marin County to Santa Rosa. I made it about half way on the 40-mile journey and woke at dawn in my red Volvo 544, sweating, the heater on full blast and the car running. We—my car and I—were by the side of the highway part way in a ditch. I don't remember getting there; my only memory was the double vision yellow lines on the pavement after leaving his house.

This was the summer I saw Anthony Quinn in "Zorba the Greek" seven straight times, mesmerized by the wonderfully rhythmic, manic, Greek dancing. I was drinking with similar abandon. After perhaps a week of non-stop carousing, one Saturday morning I woke alone in my own bed. No one else was in the house. With dream like quality, yet I knew I was not dreaming, a presence occupied the room with me. In the bedroom corner, near the door, silently, for the longest time, a figure stealthily haunted the shadows. I could not quite see its form. After an eerie amount of time passed, from the corner, my name was said. "Bob." I shuddered. It scared the shit out of me. It felt like a message.

## THE CLOCK

*the clock*

*impersonally registers*

*two fifteen*

*morning is quiet*

*and slow*

*he turns, ignoring*

*Rorschach shadows*

*cast on the ceiling*

*it is despairingly*

*alone in the long silence*

*not in just a personal way*

*without family or lover*

*or visitor breaking*

*the stillness*

*but in a larger way*

*like a cabbage growing on the moon*

*separate and incapable*

*of joining the systems around it*

*—RJG*

Not long after that, I attempted suicide. I was alone in our four-bedroom house. Life was pointless. I mooned over a magical love affair once touched but that was not to be. I lived in unending despair buoyed only by pain meds and red wine. My wife Irene was back east; she needed a break from me. Friends cared for my children, Kimberly and Judy, so young and innocent. I was lonely, with no idea how I could lift myself from this dark bog.

I switched to gin and tonics and then swallowed handfuls of pain meds, Valium and other prescription drugs. Fading fast, I called a man I knew who worked the Haight Ashbury hotline. We knew each other from encounter group experiences. He made the 60-mile ride from San Francisco to see me and got me into a hospital where my stomach was pumped. Once again I woke to hallucinations, but this time there was also a real person there—Gordon Tappan, a psychology professor who had become an emotional guide for me since my junior year of college.

I had not yet reached 30 and had a good start on being a secret drunk with a suicide attempt behind me. I was still moping about my identity. Who was I really? What were my roots? Was I Jewish? I liked a lot of qualities held by my Jewish acquaintances. I was consciously jealous of people with cultural identities, like my friend Aldo Simoni, who was so fully Italian in taste, family, and history. He knew who he was.

Somehow I managed to continue teaching, attend graduate classes, work part time, co-exist with

Irene and the kids and continue drinking. Irene and I attended counseling sessions together, enrolled in encounter groups and worked very hard to repair a tattered relationship made challenging by our respective lack of family models and my drinking. I was considered on a fast track for administrative positions in the district because of the quality of my work and the teacher-leader positions I assumed. However, I lost opportunities for promotion due to drunken behavior at a faculty retreat.

The retreat experience behind me, in 1965 I was appointed to be the teaching principal of a small elementary school located on Hamilton Air Force Base near Novato, California. Irene and I had separated. I lived in a catch-all room on the bottom floor of a two-story house Aldo had built with his father. My possessions included a record player I had used in classrooms, Harry Bellefonte songs and songs from the sound track of "West Side Story." I played these endlessly.

My finest possession was a 1950's Alpha Romeo convertible with a top that would not close. Winter days at Al's place in Windsor often produced ice on both sides of the windshield. In order to be at school long before the kids, I'd dutifully depart Windsor at 4 a.m., don socks in lieu of the gloves I didn't own, and bundled as warmly as I could manage, drive the 60 minutes to school. This got me to school early enough to do "principal work" before the teaching day began.

My second wife, Mary, and I met in a get-out-the-vote campaign in Santa Rosa where we both lived. George McCabe, who I knew as a college professor and administrator, was running to represent the sixth congressional district in California. Mary and I were instantly compatible. Furthermore, she knew my daughters because they attended school where she taught nearby in Cotati. In a prophetic kind of way, both Kimberly and Judy hung on Mary the way primary children do, when she was the yard-duty teacher. In our first year of marriage, I adopted her son, Kevin.

I was drinking but continued to advance professionally. I was recruited to serve as the director of instruction for the Belleview Union School District just south of Santa Rosa. I became the acting superintendent when the previous one took a posting in Latin America. Then, seeking a new job, Mary, Kevin and I moved to Santa Cruz where I was Director of Instruction for the Live Oak School District. It was a time of accomplishment. One teacher wrote me when I left saying she felt as if teachers there had been in the tail of a hurricane.

I was recruited again, this time to be the seventh member of a management team for a school system in Saudi Arabia. I went with Mary, Kevin and my two girls, Kimberly and Judy. Irene gave me permission to take the girls there for a year. We were to individualize instruction for the Arabian-American (Aramco) schools serving the children of oil company employees. The program was quite advanced for its time using computer assistance in reading, math, science and social studies to print daily progress statements for each student. Rather than spending time in front of classes, teachers became organizers and facilitators of small learning groups.

For me, drinking in Saudi continued to be an after-hours practice. In fact, it began to come to a head because each family owned a still in this Islamic kingdom, where purchasing (or drinking) alcohol was prohibited. I spent periodic weekends running and monitoring a still I had purchased from an engineer. We were cautioned not to drink while running the still because of two potential dangers: fire or blindness. Stills generally consisted of a stainless still cooking chamber with copper tubing carrying vapors into a condensing coil for cooling. The fittings on the copper tubing could swell or deflate allowing flammable alcohol to drop on the electric burners of our kitchen stove and start a fire. We watched for leakages and stood ready to apply flour based paste to any leaks that might occur. Equally as dangerous was going blind by not cutting the finished product to near a 90 proof alcohol level. Alcohol boils at 172 degrees 'F while it takes water 212 degrees to reach that stage so the vapors lifting off into the copper tubes were mostly alcohol. If my memory is correct, we ran the process through three times, the first boiling rendering us about 25-36 percent alcohol. The higher concentration of alcohol would be distilled again, then again, netting us at the last stage 180 proof alcohol. One must cut the product with water, back to about 90 proof. Forgetting to do so can lead to serious illness. Dave, a science teacher at the school and a heavy drinker like me, was my mentor in drinking and desert travel. We once forgot to cut the liquor back to 90 proof and got seriously ill, but not enough to get either of us to quit drinking until years later.

My expectations about drinking in Saudi were similar to that of smoking when I went to Lytton. I imagined that, since alcohol was forbidden, this would be an opportunity for me to quit drinking. But just as most of the kids smoked at Lytton, the culture of drinking was alive and well in Dhahran. In fact, I had been in the Kingdom of Saudi Arabia for no more than 20 minutes before a bottle of booze was thrust into my hand. It was the middle of the night and I had been met at the airport. "Here is a welcome-to-Saudi gift," said the man who had recruited me to Arabia, handing me a bottle of "brown." It was booze from a still. The most basic forms were either white or brown, depending on whether the liquor had been soaked in wood chips.

Geography, it turns out, was not to be the solution to my problems. I drank more and more, possibly in part because the still liquor did not produce the offsetting hangovers commercial booze did. I became concerned when at school one morning I still felt drunk –fuzzy, thick tongued and light headed. That was not OK in any job and especially not in my role as principal. When I returned to the states, I once again resolved to limit my drinking. I pretended it was manageable for a number of years, despite greater regularity and occasions of driving home so drunk I had double vision.

## NEAR THE END

Near the end I tried a number of ways to control my drinking. One of the final, and silliest, strategies was to switch to smaller glasses for my evening vodka. Like everything else, this did not work. In the final stages of my addiction, I borrowed a friend's house near Santa Cruz to edit poetry and drink in peace. It was 1975. Mostly I was writing tortured stuff born from the tensions I was feeling with my life and my second wife Mary.

## BEDMATES

*bedmates*

*trapped*

*encased in*

*same sheets*

*bound*

*by one bed*

*bodies sleeping*

*a separate sleep*

*within their lonely bed*

*love*

*or lust*

*brought them here*

*so near*

—*RJG*

This was one of them. My pattern was drink a little, write a little, and drink a little more. One evening I passed out early from my daily dose of Tanqueray Gin. I woke about 10 o'clock that night feeling depressed and desperate. I phoned AA and someone came to see me. He talked me into going to a drunk tank in Santa Cruz.

I woke the next morning in a cell smelling of booze and old men's vomit. I lay on a top bunk underneath a thin gray blanket, surrounded by unshaven, desolate and dejected men, a step away from skid row. I was frightened. What the hell was I doing here? I called Mary to come get me. Afterward I checked myself into a weeklong rehabilitation program. There I learned that my excessive drinking could not be cured by a week of "being dry." That had been my plan. Instead, I learned I had a disease, an addiction to alcohol that will power alone could not resolve. Thus I was introduced to the AA program that saved my life.

For the next three years, I attended AA meetings with fair regularity. At first I hated being there, hated the calloused hands and filthy fingernails and the people that had them. I hated the bad grammar and uneducated voices repeating stupid stories over and over again with inane phrases like "one day at a time" and "think the first drink all the way through." No shit. I was judgmental. This was way beneath my intellect. Clearly I did not belong here.

Yet I stayed, because I was afraid that if I drank again I would not be able to stop. I stayed because you don't have to like something to get value from it.

After three months agonizing in that smoke-filled room, far enough from my home and my work that I could remain anonymous, I began to hear what people were saying. I acquired a sponsor, actually two, and began working the 12-step program. I was so agnostic at the beginning that I prayed "to whom it may concern." The program took. That's a passive way of saying I worked the program, each of its 12 steps. I continued coming to meetings, I called my sponsors when times were tough, I drank gallons of coffee with other AA-ers after meetings and I kept my sobriety by mentoring others who wanted to quit drinking but couldn't. I learned basic information about alcohol and addiction and rules that made living achievable. I became ruthlessly honest with myself; an attribute the program says is essential for a person to recover from an addiction to alcohol. I worked step 4, writing pages and pages of my most secret sins. I did step 5 with Doris, my first sponsor, reading aloud what I had written. When I'd finished reading them aloud, Doris looked directly at me and said, "I don't see where you have robbed any banks." She paused. "You're forgiven. "As simple as it sounds, a great weight was lifted from me in that moment.

For several years prior to this I'd had a reoccurring dream in which two buddies and I from Lytton had murdered a man and buried him in my back yard. In the dream, the police come and start digging very close to where we had buried him. I was terrified. Every so often this same dream would occur. I would wake drenched in sweat. After going through steps 4 and 5 (made a searching and fearless inventory of myself, and admitted to God, to myself and to another human being the exact nature of my wrongs) and then 6 and 7 (I am entirely ready to have God remove all these defects of character and humbly asked Him to remove my shortcomings), the dream disappeared, never to return.

## THE CHILDREN LAUGH AND PLAY

*the children*

*laugh and play*

*while his blood runs red*

*under the ground*

*runs thick*

*under the ground*

*the children*

*laugh and play*

*running past*

*the red stain*

*spreading*

*under their trampling feet*

*the dead boy*

*lies under the schoolhouse*

*buried under*

*the rural schoolhouse*

*pushed beneath*

*the wooden floors*

*his blood*

*seeping*

*leaking*

*these many years*

*to rise*

*in the graveled*

*play yard*

*still I hide*

*lingering near the schoolhouse*

*and I will confess*

*I will confess*

*and they will take me*

*knowing I killed him*

*this young boy*

*growing under the schoolhouse*

*grasping under the schoolhouse*

*gazing under the schoolhouse*

*at me*

*—RJG*

Within months after quitting drinking, Mary and I split up. My three children were now my best reasons to stay sober. They loved me and wanted a love I could give them born of sobriety. Kimberly, the eldest, was 14; Judy was 12 and Kevin, 10. Probably my relationships with them, more than anything else, kept me in the program. They were happy to have me sober and spending time with them. I felt undeserving of their love yet incredibly grateful. On weekends the girls would come to me by bus from Santa Rosa, where they lived with their mother. I saw Kevin where he lived with his mom in Milpitas across the valley from my condo in San Carlos. Sometimes all three kids and I would get together at the same time.

Two years after I quit drinking, I stopped smoking; using ideas I'd learned from AA. So, in my 40s, I dropped a 30-year, three-to-four-pack-a-day habit. I was surprised to learn this was more difficult than quitting drinking. Nicotine leaves your body in a week or so, but for a full year, like a thief in the dark, the urge to smoke struck at unexpected moments. I learned to tell myself "not now" and the urge would pass.

The passing of alcohol brought with it the passing of parts of my former self. I experienced humility at my inability to control alcohol. I was humbled by the realization that I could not win this battle alone but needed other people, and needed to acknowledge and communicate with a higher power. I realized that I was not alone; in fact, I came to believe that some force had been taking care of me through all my drunken exploits. I thought of all the times I had ridden my motorcycle drunk in the rain or transported my three kids in the car without crashing. I learned I was not better than the people in AA meetings with dirty fingernails, just different.

I acquired basic life skills, the kinds of skills we would hope adolescents learn: to care for others, to do things simply because they needed to be done regardless of desire to do them, to take control of my spirit and attitude— manage my own weather. My decision-making processes became clearer. I no longer vacillated about simple choices—should I go to a meeting or not. And I learned to care for people who were very different from me. I experienced some measure of serenity living under the influence of the AA teachings. More serene, I realize as I write this, than I am now.

In many measures I grew up.

# CHAPTER 11

## *Meeting Sue*

### DANDELION

*the dandelion*

*casts a fluff of floating seed*

*on a warm wind.*

*somehow we had travelled like that*

*and now we come together*

*like seed and earth*

*nurturing together*

*in this meeting*

*was recognition*

*and transformation*

*of who we are*

*—RJG*

*Sue and Bob Garmston*

Fast forward to February 4, 1979, almost 30 years after I was accepted into the Hart home in Southern California as an angry, acting-out kid. Now 45, I was an elementary school principal—a high-school dropout who had worked his way to earning a doctoral degree in education from the University of Southern California. Late in the afternoon, I was at the LeBaron Hotel in San Jose to meet the woman who by March 6 I would propose to and who would, in four months (though I could not have known it then), become my wife. In retrospect, I think all my previous relationships were steps along the way to prepare me for meeting this astonishing woman. By now I had "grown up" enough to be worthy of her company.

My meeting Sue came out of a personal crisis. Since attaining sobriety, I had been living a fantasy bachelor life, with a nice condo in San Carlos, close enough to San Francisco and the coast to enjoy both, a sleek and fast Porsche and two permanent and comfortable relationships, each woman unique and right for me in her own way. The two women and I each juggled schedules to make the arrangement work—and it did work well for each of us until one fateful week when, within a space of 10 days, each of them told me she no longer liked the arrangement and wanted a monogamous relationship with me. My stomach dropped. I felt confused and let down. Overnight my comfortable and selfishly lived world changed. What do I do? Which woman? I stewed on this for several months, even taking one of the women to see a counselor with me.

## GETTING CLEAR ABOUT WHAT I WANT

The counselor told me I was working on the wrong issue. The problem, he said, was not which woman I wanted in my life. It was what I wanted in my life. He explained a strategy to deal with my dilemma. Here's what he taught me:

1) Make a list of all my needs and another of all my wants. Needs, he explained, are what are essential to survival. Food would be a need, while the kind of food might not be. At the top of my needs list was sobriety.

2) Make similar lists regarding what I would want and need in my "ideal" woman. (I remember noting that she would need to support me in caring for my children.)

3) Go about my daily living for a week or so. During that time, he said, I would be sure to think of more things to add to my lists and I did. (See the appendix for the lists that evolved.)

4) After a week, rank the things on each list in order of importance.

5) Write a goal. (This was easy for me: *Be in a monogamous relationship, the purpose of which was for me to support her in getting her needs met and she to support me in meeting mine.)*

6) Write a plan.

That last step stumped me. I had absolutely no idea how to proceed, so I wrote, "Do nothing." Weeks passed, and as they did the frequency and intensity of my contact with the two women began to decline.

About three months later, I attended a seminar led by an attractive woman from the California State Department of Education. I spoke to her at break time. "Are you attached?" I asked her.

"Yes, I am," she replied.

"That's too bad," I said, "because I could really get it on with you," I added flirtatiously. "Why don't you send me someone who has the following qualities I like in you," and mentioned several things that came to mind. She laughed, and we left on good terms.

Two months later I received a call in my office at Lakewood School. "Hi! My name is Sue. (Pause) I'm calling because I'm feeling gutsy today and a friend of mine told me about you and I am organizing a trip to Lake Tahoe to see John Denver and wondered if you would like to go along," she said breathlessly as if, were she to pause mid-sentence, she might not have the courage to continue otherwise. Long silence. I held the phone away from my body for a moment and then brought it back to my ear and said, "Sure, why not." We were instantly terrified of our reckless agreement. I phoned her later and we arranged to meet before the trip at a hotel in San Jose near where she was doing some work.

When it opened in 1974, the LeBaron Hotel immediately became San Jose's poshiest hotel. The hotel is easy to find, just a northbound turn off the First Street exit of highway 880. The restaurant and lounge, at the time of our meeting, were located on the top floor giving them a sense of privilege. The lounge could hold 30-40 people comfortably. As I recall, the afternoon sun was streaming into the windows as I waited to meet Sue. Only a few other people were in the lounge. I felt anxious.

Sue was 37, eight years younger than I. She arrived with a quiet energy, cautiously attentive.

I noticed her green eyes, which seem to disappear when she laughs, and her slight overbite, which I am still a sucker for. She was dressed professionally and appeared grounded, which she normally is. Friends later described me as the sky and her as the earth—cosmically, a perfect match.

It was crazy to think that anything might come of this. She lived in Sacramento and I in the San Francisco Bay Area, a good 90 miles apart. Yet we fearlessly spoke about ourselves: I, alcoholic, married and divorced twice, with three children and a job as principal of a nearby elementary school; she, married once and divorced, with two children living with her with her ex-husband living nearby in Sacramento. Three hours passed quickly, and as I left, my head light, I felt there was something special about this woman.

A cosmic footnote: Sue had selected my name from the Public Schools Directory, which listed four principals named Bob in the Sunnyvale School District. That she located me was a matter of chance. Coincidentally, that very month a close relative of hers, a highly successful businessman, had decided to attend a one-month live-in for recovering alcoholics.

Perhaps her knowing that helped us through our first meeting.

## THE OATMEAL CAPER

After our conversation at the LeBaron, we decided to meet once more before going on the Tahoe trip with Sue's friends. We arranged a skiing date, and, my second ex-wife, Mary, graciously let us use her house overnight before our ski day as she and her husband were away.

Sleeping arrangements were circumspect, and I took the living room couch. Wendy and Michael, Sue's kids, and my son, Kevin, were with us. In the morning I made instant oatmeal for the group, the kind that comes in individual packets. Just pour the contents in a bowl, add hot water and stir. For some reason I asked Sue several times how she liked the oatmeal: in the house that morning, on the drive to the ski resort and probably twice on the ski lifts. Each time she said she liked it. I was pleased, because it was something I often made when backpacking.

At the end of the day on the slopes, we parted, invigorated and tired. That evening I got a call from Sue who had a burning need to talk. What she revealed convinced me that I absolutely wanted to be with this woman.

"Bob, I have a confession to make," she said. "I've been dieting. When you gave me the oatmeal this morning, I didn't know how to tell you I couldn't eat it. What I wanted to tell you is that I threw it down the sink. I've been feeling terrible all day that I lied to you and just had to call and tell you the truth."

I was hooked, or as Bambi's friends would say, twitterpated. This was the girl for me.

Three weeks after we met, we knew we were going to get married. I proposed to her in my bathroom while she soaked in the tub and I sat on the toilet seat to keep her company. Her good friends cautioned her that the marriage probably wouldn't last. It has been over 31 years now. She is everything I described in the lists of the ideal mate.

# CHAPTER 12

## *Epilogue*

I am a high school dropout whose childhood was characterized by rejection, abandonment, and abuse, spending more time in group homes than with my adopted family, spending more time on the streets than most boys spend in school, yet, I went on to earn an advanced degree from a prestigious university and co-found a human development program used in most states and in twenty five countries. Later I co-developed a program to help schools develop the technical and social resources to realize continuing student improvement, also employed in many states and several countries. What had happened in those intervening years to make all this possible?

At 45, I had been sober for three years before I married Sue. Both sobriety and this marriage were watershed events after which nothing would be the same and everything would be acted out on richer playing fields. Throughout my life, both during my pre-Sue and post-Sue time I've labored on two fronts, professional advancement and personal development. The professional work had often been at the expense of the other. Even during childhood, there were indications about directions my life might turn.

## BORN TO TEACH

Marabel Beck often predicted I would be a teacher. Eleanore, too, had called me the little teacher when I was 7 or so years old. I dropped out of junior college after my first year in part because I had no goal, so no real compelling reason to stay. I accepted a job in door-to-door sales fueled by a promise of good money. The work was useful in that it taught me how to talk to people. We had a script. "Hi! I'm from the Cutco Cutlery Company. I just stopped to see if you've received your free gift? No? Well, what time this afternoon would be convenient for me to stop by with it?" The work was bad for me because, as anyone in sales knows, there can be a lot of rejections, for which I was not psychologically equipped to cope. The work finally became too much for me when I started hiring and training men how to sell and now the deceptive nature of the work became overwhelmingly evident to me.

In the year I took off from junior college to sell Cutco, an event occurred that thrust me headlong into the teaching profession. Disillusioned with sales and deciding to return to school, I took a job at the Press Democrat Newspaper to tide me over until the next semester began. The job required me to visit schools in Sonoma County and encourage fourth-, fifth- and sixth-grade kids to sell newspaper subscriptions. For each subscription, they would earn a wonderful (the promotion read) set of steak knives for their parents. I found I enjoyed talking with youngsters in those grade levels and visited large, small, rural and city schools, even the few remaining one-room school houses in the county.

But one principal, named Howard Rolfe, would not let me in his classrooms. He stood in the hallway instead and talked with me for two hours. He first explained why he would not turn his school into a commercial enterprise and then he told me what he was trying to accomplish in his school. I was thrilled with his vision and passion and knew without a doubt, for the very first time, what I was going to study in college. Later Howard Rolfe hired me as an intern fifth-grade teacher in his school. That was 1958. I had 42 kids. I made home visits to each of them. I didn't know much about teaching, but I brought love and intensity to my work. Each day my students wrote in a composition book what they had learned that day, and I read and responded to each one. Often what they recorded was about social learning or sharing personal information like "My mom had a heart attack." I became very close to each of those kids.

I learned a lot from Howard Rolfe, including an extension of the lesson I learned from the Navy not to buck city hall. I originally didn't wear ties to school, which Howard acknowledged was a professional decision of mine. However, what might be useful for me to know, he said, was that in this conservative rural community parents looked more closely at individuals who did not look like their expectations of a teacher. I wore ties from then on. It gave me greater freedom to be who I was by looking like what others expected of me. That year I had a 10-year-old boy in my class I will call Walter. His mother had dutifully brought him to kindergarten on the first day of school and then disappeared, never to be seen again.

He was an angry, rebellious little boy who would resist any direction. I had been like that, and Howard's talk with me helped me drop one of the last vestiges of my need to blatantly resist authority. Walter, however, could not do so as long as I knew him.

I was obsessively committed to serving children. My undergraduate experiences gave me a good background in the ethics and values of teaching. Ever since then I have been guided by what is best for children even when it might have been easier or more politically astute to do otherwise. By my second year of teaching Howard had moved on, and I was now a fully credentialed teacher. The new principal who took Howard's place stressed that he wanted all the desks in rows as it simplified the custodian's work. Burned by this perverted priority, I shared this information with my college advisor, who counseled me to be clear with Mr. Principal that I was in charge of the instructional program and that furniture arrangement would serve the instructional design and not clean-up needs.

The first day of school arrived, with Mr. Principal at the curb greeting the buses. He said, "Good morning, Bob. Are your desks in rows?" Well, he knew damn well they were not. I felt a familiar anger flow over me, anger at misused authority, and a sense of fear. "Mr. Principal, we need to go into your office and discuss this."

Angry with myself because I was trembling again, as I had done so long ago in the Navy, we went into his office, where I presented my stand on the desks. Many times later in my career I made stands on values. I am proud of that and critical of those who fold to pressure. With Mr. Principal, I agreed to have the kids put the desks in rows at the end of the day to make it easier for the custodian to clean. But during the day, the desks would serve the instructional purpose at hand.

Before this year was out, I was invited to apply to a forward looking and innovative school district in Marin County for the following year. I was accepted and so left my first teaching assignment to join the San Jose School District in Marin County, which sat between Novato on the north and San Rafael to the south. The Novato district has since subsumed it. Some extraordinary people staffed the district, and from them I learned things about leadership and teaching that would serve me the rest of my career.

I've recently come in contact with my mentor from those years and realize now how fortunate I was to have her guiding my development. Robin Cano's qualifications as an educator and person were exemplary. She had taught at the demonstration school at San Francisco State University and at the time I knew her she was Assistant Superintendent in charge of Curriculum and Instruction. Like me she had a challenging childhood that may have contributed to her being so good with teachers, board members and administrators. What I know about seeing the positive in people I learned from her as she shepherded me through beginning leadership experiences.

## PERSEVERANCE

Any young person will tell you that it is hard work getting through college, especially without parents or financial support, and there are many crises, both monetary and emotional, that make quitting seem like a good idea. I was not any different at three stages of my education: earning a bachelor's degree and teaching credential and the 60 units that followed that, then a master's degree from San

Francisco State, and later pursuing a doctorate when I was a principal.

The GI bill made it possible for me to attend college after the Navy; part-time work made it practical. In summer, I worked at the Press Democrat Newspaper as a relief driver for the circulation men that took bundles of papers to newsboys and newsstands in Santa Rosa and the surrounding cities. Summer mornings I was in school, afternoons I was working, and evenings I studied enough to get by unless a topic excited me. During the school year I worked a Saturday night midnight-to-noon shift on the circulation dock. I did this even while teaching. From midnight to 3 a.m. I received papers from the mailroom and loaded them into the waiting cars and trucks, and then until 10 a.m. I was on switchboard duty, fielding calls from drivers or customers who had not received papers. Then until noon, I delivered papers to the homes whose paperboy I was not able to contact.

From my smoking a couple of packs of cigarettes and drinking coffee by the gallon at night during these weekends, my mouth felt like the boxcars from the Oakland freight yards had rested there to take on coal. I ate salami and drank red wine after duty in the afternoon to cut through the awful taste in my mouth. It was hard to get to bed to catch a few hours shut eye before the midnight shift and hard to fall asleep. Sunday nights I slept like a baby, but I never seemed to get enough sleep to alleviate fatigue. My social contacts were limited with this kind of schedule and the usual parts of college life such as fraternities and other involvements were out of the question.

I had never been a good student, at least not an attentive one, so that much of what I was teaching 10-year-olds was material I felt I should have known but didn't. This, in addition to not knowing how to teach, motivated me to take evening and summer school classes. I accumulated 60 units like this in the first four years of teaching and then decided to pursue a goal other than gaining general knowledge. I then enrolled in a program leading to a master's degree and an administrative credential, resolved that I could serve as a more enlightened and humane authority than those I had grown up with. I finally succumbed to work overload and took a student loan to pay for the last 30 units so I could quit the Press Democrat job. My administrative classes were at San

Francisco State, a 50-mile commute to evening classes each way, and frankly, I was worn out.

## USC

In pursuing a doctorate, I was accepted into the University of Southern California's off-campus program to earn an initial 12 units. I was principal of the Lakewood School in Sunnyvale at the time. The first four classes were weekend courses held off campus in Sacramento, and after that, one summer residency on campus was required. I commuted for the rest of the courses. I flew from San Jose to Los Angeles once a week in time to take a 4:30 p.m. class and take advantage of the 7:30 class that followed. At first I returned after the evening class, arriving home about 3 a.m. Finally I realized I would be more rested if I stayed in a motel in LA and took the morning flight back to San Jose to go to work the next day. The financial demands were daunting. Not only was I paying for expensive units at USC, but I had plane fare, car rental and hotel charges each week as well. After several semesters, I was ready to give up, but friends urged me to keep going, and that the money would show up. Throughout this period I borrowed, borrowed and borrowed to see me through.

One significant insight at USC came during summer residency when I took two courses from the Sociology Department. Sociology was out of my field, so I studied my butt off and enjoyed learning the fresh ideas. When the grades were disclosed, I learned I had an A in each course. I remember being surprised and telling my roommate that I had pulled the wool over my professors' eyes. Almost in the same moment I said that, I heard myself denigrating my ability and effort. I was at the threshold of acknowledging my mental capacities, ability to learn and performance.

Another learning at USC came when I was awarded my doctorate. I had defended my dissertation before the dissertation committee and, as is customary, was asked to step outside the room while its members deliberated. After a while my advisor came out and sat down with me. He was silent. Finally, looking me in the eye, he said, "They don't like you." I was taken back. His comment hit me right in the face, as I am sure he intended. How else might he break through my self-perception of being superior to the curriculum and teaching in this degree program?

My attitudes were showing. I was embarrassed. After I endured for a while the silence that followed my advisor's comment, he added, "However, congratulations, Dr. Garmston. You have earned a doctorate in education."

Yet, since earning the doctorate, I've had a dream that haunts me. I chose to study for an Ed. D. instead of a Ph.D. because the latter would cost me two more classes, in money and time. I figured all I could manage was to hang on for the length of time and money required for the Ed. D. This dream comes in different forms but the plot line is always the same. I have not finished my doctorate. I have another class to take – usually in statistics. I wander about campus trying to find the administration building where I can sign up yet I have second thoughts about taking on this work again. Then I wake up, feeling like an imposter and unworthy.

## NEW GOALS

Right after my advisor's congratulations, everything turned to Technicolor Great. I ran for 5 miles on the Santa Monica Beach. I ran full out, exuberantly throwing off the pressures and anxieties related to finishing the program. I remember thinking, "Now I can learn what I want to learn." I turned my attention to neuro-linguistic programming and enrolled in a 20-day practitioner program. This turned out to be as beneficial as the doctorate in my professional pursuits. Later I attended a 30-day Master Practitioner Course.

I don't ever remember not pushing for a goal. Several Saturdays at Lytton we were brought to a roller skating rink in Healdsburg. I was not a graceful skater, nor especially skilled, but when races were held I periodically won, much to the dismay of town kids who owned their own skates and complained that they would have won had they not had rented skates that day. I would literally run around the rink slide skating until I fell, then scramble to my feet to push on. I boxed, again without skill, flailing at my opponent and winning the one formal fight in which I engaged. I was fearless in sandlot football tackling bigger kids head on and bringing them down. I got chipped teeth as testimony to my courage.

When I had two hips replaced at age 75, I was told that the better condition I was in, the easier the surgery and recovery period would be. The bone on bone pain was excruciating, yet nearly every day to prepare for surgery I took a set of hiking poles to a trail by our house and went walking. The first time out, I could move for about 5 minutes; the next day, 10 minutes. I kept pushing myself until I could walk for 30 minutes with the sticks and liberal doses of Percocet to manage the agony. Just as I pushed myself in childhood challenges I continue to do so in most aspects of my life.

## UNIVERSITY LIFE

I taught graduate courses in school administration at California State University, Sacramento and my passion, not surprisingly, was in developing school leaders who saw their authority as coming from humanistic values, and moral foundations of education rather than authoritarian role. I became a teacher of leaders, counseling students through their first administrative roles. My work after the uuniversity continued on this path, developing programs that supported individuals and groups in taking command of their own self-directed learning.

At the university I met Art Costa. We shared an office at California State University, Sacramento

California where we taught graduate students in the school of education. We formed a liason built on our respective skills, Art's in the area of developing thinking and mine in humanistic ppsychology. The result was Cognitive Coaching now used in 25 countries and administered through the Center for Cognitive Coaching in Denver Colorado. www.cognitive-coaching.com. Soon after that Bruce Wellman and I co-founded the Center for Adaptive Schools www.adaptiveschools.com, now serving educational institutions in many states and countries. Both enterprises were developed through our collaboration with educators who shared a vision with us of a world in which individuals and groups can determine their own destinies and have within them the seeds for their own self-improvement.

# CHAPTER 13

## *Transformations*

Some experiences are like placing bricks, one by one, that very slowly give strength and definition to a building. Others seem to transform, altering the very DNA of the structure. Positive ones, such as the following, have instilled strength and resiliency.

Permanent growth was not possible for me without sobriety. But while I was still drinking some incidents allowed progress in my search for identity and helped me persevere through the periods of black despair I sometimes felt. What I learned from these events stays with me now, not only as personal resources but also as sets of insights that help me understand and work with others. The first of these happened in an encounter group. I was 23. I was born again.

Encounter groups drew people who wished to grow emotionally and have more fulfilling lives. Often 12 to 20 people sat in a circle with a group leader who kept the conversation going, sometimes making observations about interactions or offering comments about the dynamics of the group. This particular event was a five-day experience at the Flamingo Hotel in Santa Rosa. Pillows were strewn about the room, and most of the participants were sitting on the floor rather than the coach or chairs. I was disclosing things about my self when a young lady, Jill, commented about what I said. I had known Jill since college, and we started teaching together the same year and in the same school. Responding to what she said, the group leader remarked, "She must love you very much to say that."

Without warning, in response to that comment, I felt as if an enormous wave engulfed my body. Light-headed, awash in sensation, I sobbed uncontrollably. Embarrassed, I ran from the room into an adjoining space, a windowless room where I sat crying loudly, mucous running, tears flooding my face, clutching my arms, holding on—and feeling my forearms–as if I had never felt them before. I felt split in half—as if there were two of me, one weeping out of control, the other observing my being born into my body—a new existence. One of the group leaders came and sat beside me, holding me but saying nothing.

This event was the most dramatic I experienced in these groups. I continued to attend these sessions throughout my 20s and into my 30s helping a new me, a more confident, grounded one emerge. Sometimes I still was achingly lonely, but often I laughed, cried, and gained insights. I enjoyed the camaraderie and the wonderful feeling of being accepted by others.

In these settings I could not help but learn about myself, about people and about the processes that bring forth authentic interactions. Hindsight suggests what research is now bearing out, that my prefrontal cortex—instrument of empathy, attunement, social connections, emotions and author of a narrative about one's life—can be developed even into adulthood. Experiences with early caregivers shape this part of the brain. I was catching up to what was probably missed as an infant.

My professional skills at "reading" people were born from this work and became seeds for the humanistic dimension of the Cognitive Coaching work I developed with Art Costa. Hundreds of hours were spent in encounter groups, sometimes with notables like Carl Rogers, Wilson Van Duson, Fritz Perls or Abraham Maslow, sometimes with professors from Sonoma State, sometimes with shared leadership self-help groups that met and camped out in a redwood grove near the Russian River at Guerneville. I became adept at reading people and often assumed leadership in these groups. In the "legitimate" encounter groups, Van Duson often used me as an authenticity scale. He'd ask me to rate a person's statement. I knew (I didn't know how I knew) with unerring accuracy the authenticity of a person's account. I could detect mixed messages or uncertainties. "A ten" I would announce rarely. More often Van asked me because he, too, sensed incongruities. I might report a "7" or an "8". Van would invite the speaker to say more. Today I know that facial muscles over which we have no conscious control reveal many emotions. I was attuned to telling the difference, perhaps from learning to read Eleanor's expressions when a child. I could tell by the set of her mouth when a rage was coming on.

Despite the time I spent feeling sorry for myself, or perhaps goaded by it, I continued to seek out therapeutic environments. An incident occurred at Wilson Van Duson's home in Ukiah, where he was the chief psychologist at the state hospital there. Sitting comfortably in Van's living room looking out over the lights of Ukiah, we were talking. "I have a feeling in the pit of my stomach," I said.

"Describe it."

I did. It was the size of a cantaloupe, and round like that, with a thick leather skin. "What's inside?"

"I don't know."

"Go into it and find out."

"I don't know how."

Van patiently encouraged me to look below the surface of this ball; finally urging me to enter it to learn what was there. Nearly 30 minutes elapsed as he entreated, I approached, he encouraged, I confessed fear, he spurred me on, and I balked. He suggested I poke just the tiniest entry hole. When I was finally able to enter, I was stunned to discover a pulsating, golden orb, its warmth filling my interior with unlimited energy. I described this to Van. "Name it," he said. I couldn't. Try as I could I could not generate a name for this marvelous life inside me.

Van then told me a story about an ancient Jewish tribe in which the rabbis were not able to pronounce the name of God in an ordinary voice. When they got close enough to God's presence, the name would burst explosively from their lips with a sound so profound even the earth would notice.

I left that session with Van feeling as if I had something worthwhile within me– something wonderful, good, alive and creative. This was a first sense of unambiguous self-worth and it measured on the Richter scale of emotions nearly as strongly as the "born again" feeling I had earlier. I was healing.

The session with Van and many encounter groups were a prelude to years of intermittent therapy. At many points in my life I sought counseling to help me through dark depression. Marabel Beck started me in this direction during my junior college years, and I came to seek and value working with someone to help me resolve my problems. During the first five years of teaching I frequently received counseling from Gordon Tappan, a psychology teacher at the University. My first wife, Irene, and I met often with Red Thomas, another professor, to try to straighten out our relationship, even though ultimately we gave up. In my seventh year of teaching I met with a Jungian psychiatrist in San Francisco who asked me if I drank too much or if I was an alcoholic. I was 32. Neither of us knew the answer. Later in AA, I was to learn that many in the helping professions are uninformed about addictions.

In the few years preceding my sobriety I did not engage in therapy but attended est seminars, which for me met similar needs. Werner Earhart, the originator of the program, broke all the rules of adult learning. Groups were large, sometimes as large as 500 people, but everyone had personal experiences. Everyone had to surrender their watch at the door, and bathroom breaks were called only when the trainer wanted to do so. Time became experiential rather than a function of numbers, and I learned that I could sustain more discomfort (no bathroom break) than I ever felt possible.

The first est experience was a two-weekend program, and I attended many seminars after that. It was in one of these that I experienced a major turning point. Werner was talking about taking responsibility for one's experiences. His point was that one could be responsible for how one responds to events. I vividly recall standing in the group of 300 participants to question him. "I don't understand," I said. He repeated the premise, but again, I did not get it. I had the feeling, even as I stood interacting with him, that what he was saying directly applied to me, yet something was blocking me from understanding.

Later that morning, Werner led a process in which participants were encouraged to go into a personal safe space and relax. He guided us in a body scan, having us pay attention to different parts of our bodies. He might start with the feet, suggesting we clench, then unclench them and feel them relax. His suggestions would move on to other parts of the body, finally including the torso, trunk and head. My breathing slowed down naturally and became deeper, every part of my body relaxed and I entered a state like a light sleep. During this process a vision emerged in which I was the sperm, swimming up the fallopian tubes, assertively entering the egg that would ultimately be my entry point into this world. I was stunned.

The image had come from nowhere. I identified with the sperm, confident, seeking, selecting, and arriving. Had I chosen this woman and man to be born to? Some believe we choose the circumstances of our birth. Or rather, was I responsible for the ways I experienced life, including being an out-of-wedlock child? Did I have choice in the ways I participated in life? Soon afterward I let go of my victim identity, realizing I had carried it for years. I was sent away from home as a child because my parents didn't want me. I could grovel in that or experience the hurt and get on with my life.

So, on another plateau of development I was again growing up. I began to accept responsibility for my choices and feelings. Rather than blame circumstances, I began to ask myself what I could learn when things did not go well.

I was driven to attend these encounter groups and workshops to survive, to quell pain, to diminish an adolescent-like embarrassment to be alive, and to find some measure of peace. I was rewarded in the sessions with insights, courage to do things differently and the sense that I belonged, even if only in transitory groups. There I could laugh, cry, interact with others and be acknowledged in these non-judgmental settings for an authentic self I could bring to the events. I believe I sought wholeness, though I wouldn't have had the concept to describe it that way at that time. I can't imagine what trajectory my life would have taken without these experiences.

I am clear that my accomplishments would have been fewer had I not invested in the growth processes that I did. In a sense, my mother's voice, the voice that said I was inadequate, inherently bad and unworthy of love pushed me to overcome those destructive messages. I thought that by self-improvement and achievement I could render the voice quiet. Such voices are not silenced easily. I get whispers even today.

## WORKSHOPS

Ever seeking growth, Sue and I went to many seminars by the est organization devoted to communication and human development. Sue also attended a workshop by

Angeles Arrien, which was valuable for her, and with Sue's encouragement I attended a workshop by her the following year. I was unprepared for what I got.

Angeles Arrien is a cultural anthropologist, an award-winning author, an educator, and a consultant to many organizations and businesses. She lectures and conducts workshops worldwide, bridging cultural anthropology, psychology, and comparative religions. The session I attended with her was a five-day residential program in the high desert in Arizona. Participants were to acquire skills, tools, practices and experiences in the way of the warrior, the healer, the visionary and the teacher. These are the cornerstones for what she describes as the Four Fold Way.

Thirty to forty people sat on the floor around the edges of a circular room. Angeles was one member in the circle. She told stories and gave information. Talking, laughter, and sometimes tears were experienced . On this occasion she instructed us to go outdoors and after spending time alone to build something out of rocks of personal significance. I built a mausoleum holding the remains of my birth mother.

I don't know where the idea came from. Perhaps it was stimulated by conversations in the circle.

After returning to the room and speaking about our experiences outside, Angeles talked about different levels of consciousness and that we were about to enter a different level through an ancient practice of drumming. She said that when awake, most people exhibit brain wave patterns that are either beta or alpha. Betas are those associated with day-to-day wakefulness. These waves are the highest in frequency and lowest in amplitude (largeness or distance from mean point) and also less regular than other waves. During periods of relaxation, while we are still awake, our brain waves become slower, increase in largeness and become more alike. These types of waves are called alpha waves. For example, such brain waves are often associated with states of relaxation and peacefulness during meditation and biofeedback.

Certain patterns of drumming induce alpha waves. Out came the drums. We were asked to lie on the floor, relax our bodies, close our eyes and select a male and female guide to join us in this journey. I struggled to locate someone in my memory that I wanted to do this exercise with. I chose William

Shakespeare for his wisdom and a female figure for feminine strengths. Grrr. These figures were not right. Instead, at the last moment, I chose my biological mother and father.

I settled into the rhythms of the drumming. I relaxed even deeper. The beat seemed to be coming from inside me. My mind drifted. Shortly afterward I felt the presence of my birth mother residing within one side of my body and my birth father in the other, head to toe, lying there inside me. They stretched their hands over my chest to touch one another's hands. I wept.

For me this was an incredible healing process, and the image and experience stayed with me several weeks. I imagined that my birth parents loved each other. Together they had expression in me. I feel complete just thinking about it and am reminded that Carl Jung, the most influenctial psychiatrist of the twentieth century, said that life is about integrating our many parts. It was calming.

I have no way of knowing if this contributed to my being more open to the importance of family, but I know it coincided with development in that area.

## SIERRA GHOSTS

I resolved to take a final backpacking trip before marrying Sue, a solo trip a perfect way for me to enjoy my last act of independence and reflect on the life choice I was making. It turned out to be more adventure than I had sought.

I left the San Francisco Bay area at night and headed for Pinecrest, where I planned to sleep at the trailhead and start hiking fresh in the morning sun. Moving through the Gold Country, then up Highway 28 past Tuolumne and Train Harte toward Dodge Ridge, I traveled with my thoughts. My good friend and AA sponsor, Bud, had just died as a result of a motorcycle accident. He was an Alan Watts-quoting, truck-driving, gold-prospecting free spirit who had pulled his bike in front of an oncoming truck. We who knew him wondered if this had been his way out of addictions he could not overcome. He lay in a coma for a month. Each time I visited the hospital I could feel his presence when I stepped off the elevator onto his floor, except the last time. He was not there. He had "passed" the night before.

Even though someone has died, the relationship lives on in our heads. I'd been taught that to complete a relationship, I needed to finish all the undelivered communications. I began that conversation that night with Bud, speaking out loud of my love for him, my upsets, my appreciation, and my betrayals. Tears flowed as I emptied my heart, hiding nothing. The sense of his presence was so real that twice I glanced into the passenger seat of the Volkswagen camper expecting to see him sitting there. After a while, the intensity passed. I finished the drive in peace, not knowing that this was to foreshadow a more intense confrontation in the mountains.

On the morning of the next day, I prepared the final organization of my pack, secured the van and set off for the trail. I carried a light pack, about 40 lbs, and forded the early morning creek at trailhead to set off into the Emigrant Wilderness, a 900,000-acre area of land with a majestic range of mountains, lush meadows, mountain lakes and canyons between lying between Lake Tahoe and Yosemite. Elevations range from 5,000 to 11,500 feet, and the beginning of any backpacking trip seems inevitably to be up. I doggedly trudged upward, pausing periodically to catch my breath and adjust my pack. After three hours or so, the terrain flattened and I traversed a ridge with more gentle rises and falls. The hardest part of this day was done. In the next four hours the pack became a part of my body, I felt the rhythm of legs and feet striking the terrain, my boots would form more tightly around my feet and I was thoroughly into the experience. Enjoying the trail now, I listened to bird-calls and periodically looked up from picking my feet between rocks to enjoy the green trees, distant vistas and occasional deer scampering away from me. That evening it rained. I pitched my tent near the shores of Chewing Gum Lake. Having trenched around the outside to allow for run off, I spent a reasonably comfortable night.

The morning was brisk but clear. I headed east for a few hours, stopping by a rushing brook for a lunch of soup and crackers. The day had warmed but was now turning colder. I decided to cut cross-country to a plateau at about 9,000 feet. I could sleep there, I reasoned, and head for higher country the next day. The ascent led me through sparse trees and occasional underbrush. The going was hard and I perspired heavily. The chill in the air increased, and I began to encounter drizzle. I started to worry. The summit was nowhere in sight, and I was alternately sweating and freezing, a bad combination on a solo hike with uncertain surroundings. I wasn't sure where I was and began debating with myself what to do. Should I press on or try to bunk down here on the side of the hill? My movements became less certain, my thinking more sluggish.

By the time I was close to the top, I was shivering uncontrollably and knew I had to get warm. Stories of hypothermia, which kills hikers, were in my head. I fumbled the tent out of my pack and struggled to get it anchored onto the forest floor. When it was partially upright, I got inside and awkwardly wormed into my sleeping bag. Lying on my stomach, I fired the stove, and heated soup. As time passed, I finally stopped shivering, and feeling warmth return to my body, I snuggled deeper into the bag and slept.

The next day I awoke to warming skies and cumulous clouds against a blue sky. I made coffee and had oatmeal for breakfast. After breaking camp, I continued cross-country, now sure of my whereabouts. A two-hour hike took me to a trail juncture at Whiteside Meadow, where I sat, broke out trail mix and water and studied my topo map. Satisfied that I had deciphered the route accurately, I set off. It continued to be a fine early summer day. When I rested to meditate on the side of a trail, a curious hummingbird fluttered before my nose. It was nice to have the company, but my meditative skills were no match for this type of intrusion. Then I continued on my hike, walking most of the day.

As evening fell I found myself in a valley that shouldn't be there, at least it shouldn't be configured the way it was according to my reading of the map. I studied the terrain, consulted the map and walked to different points of the valley to gain perspective. I was lost but not too troubled because I knew I could retrace my steps the next day, so I went in search of a suitable campsite. Camping by water is romantic but not always practical. The sound of a running stream can distract from sleep and mask other sounds. I was far enough north of Yosemite to not have to worry about bears.

After I set up camp and ate dinner, I was aware of a presence in the valley. It was strong enough that I went searching for other campers. I searched the perimeters of the tiny valley to the west and the east, explored areas behind stands of trees, and walked around granite boulders but nowhere could I find anyone. Still, the sense of someone being there persisted. I even tried some "halloos" in my strongest voice but got no response.

I climbed into the sack that night with some apprehension. I don't mind being alone, but to be alone yet feel the presence of hidden guests is uncomfortable. That night I dreamed of John Garmston.

I awoke the next morning feeling John's presence. I broke camp and headed back up the steep trail that brought me here. John was on my mind. I decided to try to "complete my relationship" with him by saying everything to him that had been left unsaid. I told him that I loved him. I told him that I had wanted his love. I told him I realized he wasn't demonstrative but still wished he had talked to me more or even put his arm around my shoulders. I told him how pissed I was that he had let the Lytton authorities dictate his actions when I was being punished. I felt robbed that he agreed not to take me with him on the trip he had planned. I told him how devastated I was. I told him how his handling of the burned football hurt and that it was a cowardly thing for him to do.

Unlike the response I got in Milpitas when I asked Eleanore what life was like for her when I was a child, John was silent through all this. I was verbalizing all this stuff out loud. The more I talked, the more distressed I got. The more distressed I became the more I cried with the racking sobs and mucus from my nose running over my lips. I was briefly aware of what a picture this must make, a grown man with a pack on this back, talking out loud and blubbering at 10,000 feet on a trail in the Sierras. Thank God I did not pass any hikers that day.

Much later, while writing this book, I asked John what life was like for him when I was a child. I was stunned to hear the response from somewhere within me—"I never wanted her to die." At that moment I realized that his life was probably consumed with grief for a good two years when I was an infant, mourning the loss of the woman with whom he had adopted a child.

Curiously, after this experience in the Sierras I found I was referring to John as father. I had never been able to do this before. I continued to do so until my entire world was rocked at age 60.

## A LYTTON REUNION

When I was 50, married to Sue, living in Sacramento and teaching at the university, out of the blue I got a phone call. "Hi," the caller said. "Can you guess who this is?" I had no idea, but found out that it was Jack had been one of my buddys at Lytton. Jack, Gilbert and I were the "Three Musketeers." We had run away from the home frequently, built the tree house in the hills, started the fire behind the school house, drank red wine, stolen cigarettes from other kids and generally were compatible trouble makers. He called to tell me there was a reunion at Lytton. Was I interested in attending? Hell, yes! I met him there.

Not only was Jack there, but my first wife, Irene, my social worker Marabel Beck, and a few other kids I had known were there as well. Jack and I toured the grounds, visiting the gym and seeing the names and initials carved into the door on the projection room. We toured the cottage where we slept, looked in places in the big house where we were not allowed as kids and caught up with what each had been doing since Lytton. Jack, I heard, had been to Leavenworth, was addicted to heroin and broke the habit.

He complained that a white man his age couldn't get a job and the world was stacked against him.

It was like I was 14 again. The jokes, the put downs rolled from our lips as if we were still kids at the home. He was skinny as he had always been and as scheming. Before we left that evening he confided in me that he had stolen the door from the projector room and was going to take it home.

Never has the expression "There but for the grace of God" seemed more appropriate. Jack evidenced the same mental set, attitudes, and immaturity we both had when we were kids. Somehow I had developed. Jack had not. I thought about this after the visit.

Later I met a Folsom Prison guard at the gym where I work out. I asked Skip what was the difference between the people behind bars and the general population. "You mean the way they think?" he asked. "Yeah."

"Well, for starters they are all innocent," he said. "Nothing is their fault, they blame everyone else for their predicaments, they are the product of a warped society. Impulse control is another issue" he said.

"They have none. Maybe it's something in the genes or maybe it's about impulse control. Maybe there are some born without that switch."

"Yeah, I said. "Or don't know how to use it."

He was describing Jack.

Another thing that took place at the Lytton reunion stayed with me for days. Several of us were standing on a porch off the big house. It was the first time anyone called me Bob instead of Bobby. It was also on this porch that Kitty M. had pinched and saved a cigarette butt of mine in a display of adolescent love. Standing on this porch now at the reunion, a woman asked me what I was doing. When I told her I was teaching at the University she said, "Well, we always knew you were smart."

Her comment struck me dumb, not just for the rest of that evening but for quite some time afterward. Smart. I had never considered myself smart. That others had done so shocked me. As I reflected about this over the next few days, I came to several conclusions. One is that being smart, whatever precisely that meant, wasn't my fault. I could take no credit for it. It wasn't something I developed but rather had. (I did not know the research to the contrary at that point.) Being smart, I reasoned, was like having blue eyes. Not my fault either.

The other conclusion I reached was that I had wasted my potential. If I were really smart, I would have done more with my life, with my career.

## CARING AND EMPATHY

Having a variety of experiences increases the numbers and types of people one can understand or have some empathy for. For example, the fact that I have tattoos led to a connection I might never have made without them. This experience led me to be grateful, once again, for the unusual nature of my childhood.

My tattoos are a product of India ink and a pin held by my buddy Gabby Moore rat-a-tat-tatting on my skin late at night in the bathrooms in Sonoma Cottage. I was 14. "RJ" went on my right shinbone for Robert John, "Bob" over a gang mark on my left shoulder and "HHS" for Healdsburg High School on my other shoulder. On the back of my right hand a large question mark inscribed over the same gang mark and on my left hand, an "L" on my index finger and an "O" on the next. What might have turned into the classic jailhouse LOVE on the fingers of one hand and HATE on the other stopped there. During my physical for a teaching credential, the examining doctor advised me to remove the tattoos on my hands. "No," I told him. "I want to remember where I came from." Much later in life I had the ones on my hands removed with a laser at the encouragement of Alice Hart, my final adoptive mother.

In a recent visit to have blood drawn, I had a conversation with the middle-aged Latino woman taking my blood. On the webbed space between her thumb and pointing finger, an unrecognizable and faded tattoo caught my eye. "When did you get this?" I asked. A long time ago was her reply. I told her that I had some tattoos on my hands when I was 14. She smiled then, her entire demeanor opening up.

"I was 16 when this went on," she said. "We used ink and a straight pin to put it on."

"That's exactly the process we used–India ink and a pin–punch-punch-punch," I told her, miming the thrusting of the pin repeatedly into the skin. "I had a buddy put Healdsburg High school on this shoulder. Can you believe? I had it covered over in the Navy."

"Yeah," she said. "This one," she added, pointing to her hand again, "covers up my boyfriend's name that I put on there when I was 16." We both laughed.

"Decisions we make," I said.

"Yeah. I have one up here too, she said," pointing near her right shoulder but up higher onto the ridge of her back. "You know sometimes when someone comes in to get their blood drawn from me, they see the tattoos and tell me I am evil."

I expressed surprise.

"Yeah! One person said any dirtball that puts a tattoo on another dirtball is not worth spit. A couple walked out, saying I'm not having my blood drawn by someone with tattoos."

We talked about understanding that people can have attitudes but that it was beyond our comprehension why they would express them so rudely. But not everyone did that. "You know," she said, "I had a 90-year-old woman come in for her second blood test. And when she arrived she pointed to her upper back and said excitedly, 'Look, I got a tattoo here since seeing you.'"

## PRESUMING POSITIVE INTENTIONS

Just as I formed a good relationship with the woman drawing blood, that same quality of empathy is easiest when knowing something about another person's struggle. Empathy is one hallmark of a good teacher and after my first year of teaching "problem" boys were routinely assigned to my class because I was effective with them, not because of superior pedagogy or special discipline practices but because my heart went out to them as I identified with their stories or circumstances. I could find the good in them and not be distracted by the problematic behaviors. I could be nonjudgmental yet deal with the behaviors that needed to be corrected. Today I am predisposed to be open to generous interpretations of behaviors and act, when necessary, without blame.

Yet every so often, I presume the worst about someone only to find out later that I have been wrong. Sue and I contracted with a painter to install a new window and paint. He didn't show up. We didn't hear from him. Grumbling, I blamed him and the entire painting industry for not having more responsible people. We had been burned by a painter once before and I was assigning the same attributes to this guy. Two days later he reached us to tell us his mother, who lived in another town, had experienced a heart attack. He had rushed to her side and been with her the entire time.

This is a lesson I have to frequently relearn. People have good reasons for their behavior usually associated with attempts to take care of themselves. This is true even when the behaviors are counterproductive or work against them. This has become one of the tenets in the Adaptive Schools work—to presume positive intentions.

To presume that others have positive intentions meant becoming less judgmental about myself. I was late in developing some capacity at this, largely due, I think, to a lifelong struggle with depression.

## BEYOND DEPRESSION: LEARNING TO LOVE

Perhaps the most significant and difficult changes I've had to make since marrying Sue are dealing with depression and learning to embrace family. The two are related because my depression at times fostered volatility and mood shifts, making me hard to live with.

I suspect I've been depressed most of my life. The alcohol was, in part, a way to deal with it. In the early stages of writing this book my primary doctor detected that I was appearing lifeless and depressed to her and wondered if my anti-depression medications were working. I met with a psychiatrist to discuss this. His diagnosis was "without a doubt" that I am bipolar. Fortunately I have a comparatively mild form of this disorder. In my case, the depressive periods are characterized by low energy, inability to focus, irritability, feelings of worthlessness and withdrawal from people. My lighter stages manifest by elevated mood, hyperactivity, sustained and intense work periods, reckless behavior and a tendency to be easily distracted.

I'm pretty sure I am also ADHD, having an attention-deficit hyperactivity disorder, the name of a group of behaviors found in some children and adults. Where one diagnosis starts and the other one leaves off I'm not sure. But I know these ADHD behaviors describe me very well. I have difficulty following instructions (ask my wife), often don't listen, don't pay attention to detail, and am disorganized. My desk looks like a hurricane struck. In this mess I lose books, papers and projects. In other parts of the house I lose personal belongings. I forget things and am easily distracted. What a burden I must have been for Eleanore.

However, there is a possibility I owe my professional success, in part, to being ADHD. It has caused me to work harder than I suspect others do in order to learn new material, to compose, and to design workshops. Without the need to struggle, I may have worked less and accomplised accordingly.

## AFFECTS ON OTHERS

For nearly 31 years now, Sue has been saint-like in dealing with these traits of mine. This is not to say that she has not been angry, hurt or blaming at times. It does mean she has worked to understand, cope and help me manage some of these behaviors.

Those who work with me have had to overlook these patterns and carry on despite the disruptive nature these aspects can have to planning, problem solving or performing. My closest friend and partner, Art Costa, has also been patient and forgiving of these qualities as we have written books, led groups and conducted seminars together.

At home, Sue has been the major recipient of my mood swings, distractibility and anger. Michael and Wendy, who were 12 and 9 when we married, also suffered from my fury. I remember on more than one occasion driving in our Volkswagen bug convertible when I would slam on the breaks and yell at the kids to be quiet.

Sue and I were married in 1979, the year after I completed my doctorate and left public education to do professional development in the private sector. The first two years of marriage were the roughest. I've heard it said that if you want to be happy for an hour, rest. If you want to be happy for a day, go fishing. If you want to be happy for a month, get married. Our first thirty days—and beyond—were ecstatic. Yet in blended marriages such as ours, the authority regarding children rests with the original parent. The newcomer has none. We proactively hired a family counselor to meet with the four of us for "family meetings." On hindsight we probably knew more than this young lady about psychology and family dynamics, but it was helpful to have a neutral ear in the conversation. Much later I learned that the kids would deliberately set me up to get me mad. They tease me about it today.

We have had a strong marriage but not always an easy one. Several times I exploded on vacation, once in Vietnam and another time in Alaska, another in Athens and another in Berlin. Part of the problem has been dealing with antidepressants over the years. In Vietnam I learned the hard way that Prozac interacted badly with Melatonin, the drug used to counteract time-zone problems. I've never taken it since. In Alaska, I decided to stop taking my meds to see if I could get along without them. Both occasions were disasters.

I was teaching at the university when I first took Prozac. I was probably 53. I was experiencing high stress at work and was bringing it home. Both Art and I worked full time at our responsibilities with graduate students and at the same time were flying all around the country conducting Cognitive Coaching seminars. At the time my wife, Sue and I owned a bed-and-breakfast inn in Sacramento that she managed while working almost full time for the state Department of Education. In addition to everything else, I was traveling frequently to Fresno (there is no easy way to get there) teaching instructional skills to earn money to manage the shortfalls from the B and B. Both of us were exhausted. A therapist I was seeing suggested one day that antidepressant medications might be helpful. I had lived over half a century before someone noted I had the classic signs of depression.

I will always remember the first benefit of Prozac. I was on the back porch feeding our family cat when, without warning, she reached up with her claws and dug into the back of my hand. I felt my anger rise on one side of my body, move in a complete arc, and then suddenly, like the snap of a finger, it was gone. I was astonished, delighted! The electric arc I felt in my body was much like the arc I experienced sniffing gas tanks as a kid.

What got us through a multitude of challenges were two agreements we made at the beginning: Bob has 100 percent responsibility for anything that goes wrong. And no matter how hard it gets, we will never, ever quit—we are stuck with each other.

The responsibility agreement has saved our bacon on a number of occasions. Unstated in the agreement is that Sue also bears 100 percent responsibility for what goes wrong. It only takes one of us in a heated conversation to say, "Wait a minute. I must be doing or saying something wrong here. I'm not sure I get it. Would you explain it to me?" and like magic, the air escapes from any toxic balloon we have constructed and we then work on hearing each other.

Sue and I worked on our relationship and I worked on me, periodically going for counseling. We both learned ways to cope with my anger. One effective strategy she used was to say to me, "Bob, how long are you going to be mad?" I would reply, "One minute," and then gloriously emote for 60 seconds before stopping. We both laugh about that today.

What we don't laugh about is that my depression reoccurs. Even while writing this section of the book, a major depression has taken hold of me. I am morose, irritated and annoying, lose energy and am miserable to be around. I'm working with a psychiatrist to find the right adjustment to my medications, am arranging further counseling and will do a repeat session with Angeles Arrien searching for some inner peace medicinally and spiritually. Sue says my redeeming feature is that I never give up.

## FAMILY

After John died, Eleanore was a loner, living alone in sparsely furnished one-room apartments and having contact with almost no one. She attended movies and read books but otherwise led the life of a hermit. My childhood memories of extended family are sparse. I recall one occasion when Eleanore invited her brother to dinner at our San Diego house on Marlborough Street. I hid under the table and was severely reprimanded for that behavior. On another occasion Eleanore and I visited a relative in Sacramento. It was winter in a yet-undeveloped track. Muddy dirt roads connected the houses. I remember playing with Adrienne, a girl about my age. We got into the giggles and could not stop. Other than meeting Babs and living in Oakland with Aunt Violet and Great Uncle Hans, that is the sum total contact

I had with Eleanor's family. John's family was never mentioned. During my Lytton years, family time consisted of a visit at Christmas and another during the summer. On those occasions, tension presided in the house.

Sue values family. She maintains regular contact with her brother, sister and stepmother. She helps organize extended family reunions every five years in which 30 or so people come together for a week. In our home she is the matchmaker, bringing our kids together in rented premises for summer and other holidays. She invented "Children's Christmas," at which all the little ones come for a dinner party and games. For several years she "sat" for Sean and Ethan when they went to school near us. Afternoons would be homework time, snack time and games. They love each other, in part, I believe, because of all the opportunities Sue created for them to be together. She is the person that reminds me to call Kevin or my girls. She shops for them all year long putting things aside for birthdays or Christmas. On my 75th birthday she organized the rental of a huge home in the Tahoe area to house friends and family for a week.

I lived with Wendy and Michael long enough, and have cared for each enough, that both feel good about me. Their birth father lives in Oregon, so I am their "other father" in their minds. They both love me and are close to me. Once at a party for Sue I remarked that I was broken goods. "Yes," Wendy said, "but Havilland china." I appreciated that. Gradually I get reminders that, at the core, I must be all right.

I've felt depressed and lonely at Christmas until very recently. I remember walking on Healdsburg streets as a kid and seeing houses lit up with holiday decorations and lights. I tried to imagine what it must be like in those homes. I dragged the Christmas despondency into my marriage with Sue. Guess what, as my daughter Kimberly would say: Sue loves Christmas, and other holidays.

In the beginning I resented the time spent in decorating the tree—which would become, I reasoned, undecorated in a few weeks. I was often morose, even on Christmas morning opening packages. Try as I might, I was unable to overcome the burden of my history.

Gradually this changed. Sue is relentless in her enjoyment of holidays. I began to take pleasure in setting up the electric train running beneath the tree. I participated with friends in Christmas parties where Santa (Ed Riley) would appear in full outfit with a sack over his back. I began to look forward to those events.

Today I often don't know when Memorial Day is about to happen because holidays aren't on my radar. But Christmas, thanks to Sue, I appreciate.

## COMING HOME

Each Easter Sunday finds our family at Dillon Beach. We rent a home for the weekend. This last year one of those special, once-in-a-lifetime events occurred. We sat on the deck of the rented house. The afternoon sun warmed my bare legs and face, a welcome change from the fierce winter winds battering us earlier. My son, Kevin faced me in the intimate circle. To his right, my daughter Judy and to his left sat her older sister Kimberly. We were talking about what to do with my ashes when I die. Love, like an electric current, connected us all. I commented on it first, and my children remarked that they felt it too. I felt as if we were bound together as one. The others also felt it. It was almost as if we were being embraced, covered and held by a loving presence larger than ourselves. Later I realized that we were the last remaining family members of this tiny unit, Kevin's mother having died years earlier and Irene, mother to the girls, lying mentally incapacitated by dementia, unable to even recognize her daughters when they visit her in the residential care facility where she lives.

This moment was worth more than my history, my credentials, accomplishments, adventures, good phases and bad, exultations and disappointments, joys and travails. I am complete as if nothing before has ever existed nor mattered, at least for now.

## POSTSCRIPT

In January 2011 the Los Angeles School Board

designated a school in South Central Los Angeles, home of the LA riots, as

Estrella Elementary—A Garmston—Costa Academy

# APPENDIX A

While writing this, I wondered if I could find the lists of wants and needs that culminated in my meeting with Sue. I did. Not only were these lists in my files (see below), I also found nine goals that were stimulated by this. I am including them here to provide an example of the kind of thinking involved in this process of listing my needs in general and then my needs in terms of an ideal mate. I am also including them because I am amazed at what has occurred in my life in relation to the goals I wrote. When I recorded these I was still an elementary school principal with no prospects for doing work beyond that. Yet, these goals I wrote in 1979 have been achieved many times over. I think there is a power in goal setting, as illustrated in this experience that exceeds rational explanation and is almost magical. First are my two lists of needs and then my related goals.

Needs

| In General | Ideal Mate |
|---|---|
| • Sobriety<br>• Know who I am<br>• Guts to be who I am<br>• Have a mate<br>• Self-honesty<br>• Live in integrity<br>• Be excited by my job<br>• Be creative in my job<br>• Have alive, intelligent friends<br>• Time alone<br>• Quiet time<br>• Be physical<br>• Be trim, healthy, vigorous, attractive<br>• Friends who love me<br>• My children love me<br>• Satisfying sex<br>• Clean, orderly, attractive home | • Seen as attractive by others<br>• Gives me unconditional love<br>• Works in creative/ professional field<br>• Has time for me<br>• Supports relationship with my kids<br>• Would need me<br>• Would be intelligent<br>• Would be sensual<br>• Would live in integrity<br>• Would be emotional<br>• Tells it the way it is<br>• Would want me to need her<br>• Would be gentle<br>• Open communicator<br>• Wants time for herself<br>• Contributes critical thinking to ideas |

| | |
|---|---|
| • Honesty with mate<br>• Keep and strengthen my AA family<br>• Life plan or direction<br>• Have adventures<br>• Receive adulation<br>• Have a quiet home<br>• Have money enough for comfort<br>• Make restitutions to those I've harmed | • Can trust her to be monogamous<br>• Knows who she is<br>• Has the guts to be who she is<br>• Already established in work field<br>• Growing<br>• Happy<br>• Keeps clean attractive house<br>• Supports me in limited eating<br>• Has satisfaction in her job |

Nine Goals

1. Be in a monogamous relationship, the purpose of which was for me to support her in getting her needs met and she to support me in meeting mine.

2. To be a professional entrepreneur, workshop leader, college teacher, consultant and trainer.

3. To create my own work schedules.
4. To be singly at today's equivalent of $30,000 annual income, jointly at $50,000. (These are 1979 figures.)
5. To stay in a state of integrity and growth.
6. To acquire a home with a view and a den for me.
7. To work part time at age 55.
8. To retire at age 60.
9. To have a balance among play, goal behaviors, God, alone time and together time.

Looking back, though I was not consciously driven by or working on this set of goals, I became a university professor, developed new courses in educational administration, published six books, co-founded two training organizations with international reach, and worked in Africa, Australia, Asia, Europe, North America and South America as a consultant and trainer. I've been fortunate to trek in the Himalayas, boat and hike along the Amazon, overnight with hill tribes in Thailand, travel by elephant, raft and canoe, scale

Mt. Whitney, climb Mt. Kilimanjaro and go on safari, many times, in Africa. The goals I did not achieve were related to part-time work and retirement, waiting until age 75 to semi-retire.

*Marabel Beck*

*Alice and King Hart*

# APPENDIX B

## *1950 and 1951*

*Excerpts of Correspondence Regarding Bob at the Harts*

Communications are from:

- Marabel (Mrs. Marabel Beck, Social Worker at Lytton),
- Alice (Mrs. Alice Hart, mother at the home at which Bob has been placed and
- Bob's father (Lt. John J. Garmston USN and mother (Mrs. Eleanore Garmston).

These excerpts are from letters related to my time at the Harts in 1950 and 1951. They reveal Mrs. Beck's unrelenting efforts on my behalf, some of the problems the Harts contended with by housing me, Mrs. Beck's assessments of me and my parents' attitudes.

I left Lytton and arrived at the Hart's home in June 1950. By September, I had become too difficult for the Harts to handle. Many letters flew back and forth and for a time I must have left the Harts and stayed with the Becks before returning to Leucadia. I left the Harts in February 1951 and joined the Navy in March.

September 16. My father writes advising that a civilian doctor provide dental work. Bob should continue in high school, and make earning secondary to school and use income for clothing and incidentals.

September 18. Marabel writes to the Harts about Bob's behavior and suggests that we request of his parents to have Bob return home. Marabel observes that *Bob's behavior is characteristic of youngsters whose rejection comes early —almost a total inability to attach positively to adults and other kids and* that the Harts should not feel they have failed Marabel.

September 26. Marabel writes to the Harts—Bob's behavior seems to be running true to what most foster parents experience: ups and downs.

October 5: Marabel advises the Harts about a trip Bob wants to make. She suggests he might be growing away from the old crowd and that Bob's parents want him to finish school; failing that, he should enlist in the Navy.

November 1: Marabel commiserates with the Harts about another Lytton kid who dropped in to visit Bob at the Harts and stayed. Jim was problems with a capitol "P"— while in Leucadia the two boys ran on the streets at night drunk on muscatel wine, Jim planned to rob the bowling alley, and played wild shooting games with a .22 gun. He was a supreme con and sponge.

November 1. Marabel sends a handwritten note to Alice regarding Bob's behavior. She thinks she should write Bob about his situation (parents and threat of Navy) and asks Alice's opinion.

December 5: Marabel writes to Bob counseling him on his behavior choices. She advises that personal problems need to resolve around "fact" and not what one would want the situation to be. She advises that what the Harts request of Bob sounds reasonable and going home will not solve these problems. It might become easy for you, she says to Bob, to constantly excuse yourself because of external situations.

December 5: Marabel responds to Alice's letters. Bob's mother's rejection is deep but disguised. Bob has always shut out discussion about his family and walled himself in. Last year he received a letter from his mother in which she practically told him he was not wanted at home. Marabel has picked up information from other Lytton kids he has been in touch with that Bob is probably drinking.

Marabel tells the Harts they have been more successful than they realize. She thinks his insistence on carrying out his own wishes is a way of trying to assert his own individuality. The whole matter of who he is and why things have happened to him are uppermost in his mind.

December 8: Eleanore writes over John's signature (I can tell her writing) that their house is far too small to take Bob in and hopes he can finish the school year in San Diego.

December 11: Marabel shares her correspondence with the Garmstons, noting their reluctance to assume responsibility. She notes her concern that Bob will remain trapped in his own rationalizations.

December 11: The Harts have requested that Bob leave, preferably by the 18th of this month.

December 11: Marabel lets Bob know his parents have requested his return.

January 9: (This letter is puzzling to me. I must have gone north to stay with the Becks for a period of time. ) Marabel says that Bob wants to return to Leucadia and help the family with part-time jobs and in other ways. Up until recently he thought he was wanted at his parents' home. While Bob is resistant to direction, in terms of other severely rejected kids, he appears to function amazingly well. Bob appears to be facing the fact that his parents want to drop out of the picture and he is pretty much on his own. He turned 17, 45 days ago.

January 18: Marabel writes that Bob's father is forwarding money for Bob to return. Bob may need the Harts' help in meeting the situation.

***February 1:*** Handwritten note from Marabel. Bob's father (angrily) wants him home immediately.

Feb 14: Marabel tells Alice her file shows Mrs. Garmston's expression for Bob and his father and Mr. Garmston's hatred for Mrs. Garmston. She hopes things work out for Bob.

March 14: Handwritten note to the Harts from Marabel. Bob is enlisting in Navy. Didn't last long in Massachusetts.

## 1950 and 1951

## Correspondence Regarding Bob at the Harts

Communicating are the following:

- Marabel (Mrs. Marabel Beck, social worker at Lytton),
- Alice (Mrs. Alice Hart, mother at the home at which Bob has been placed), and
- Bob's father (Lt. John J. Garmston USN) and mother (Mrs. Eleanore Garmston).

*16 September 1950*

*431 Dewey Street*
*West Springfield, Mass.*

*Dear Mrs. Beck,*

*In answer to your letter of September 7th, concerning Bob's dental needs. Please make arrangements to have the work done by a civilian dentist, and send the bill to Lytton to be reimbursed by me. There is no Naval dental service for dependents.*

*We feel very earnestly that Bob should continue High School, do as well as he can in his studies, try to develop an interest in finishing school work toward graduating, and confine his earnings to after school and weekend work. There is little question that, though he may have to discipline himself to the routine of school work and activity, he will feel gratified that he did keep to it to earn a High School diploma.*

*In the meantime, it should develop a sense of responsibility and independence and afford him a sense of satisfaction to do what he can in the way of clothing purchases and some incidental expenses, such as school needs.*

*Sincerely yours,*
*John J. Garmston*

*September 18, 1950*

*Mr. and Mrs. C. K. Hart*
*Box 286*
*Leucadia, California*

*Dear Alice and King:*

*Your letter arrived on Saturday with the news about Bob. I think in view of all the difficulties you are having with Bob and the fact that neither Lytton nor you have any kind of legal control that it is probably best that we now request the parents to have Bob return home. This will mean, I believe, that you will have to tell Bob that you have been concerned about him and have written me in regard to the difficulties you have been experiencing. You may refer to the fact that I have previously discussed with Bob the fact that I would be keeping in touch with you in regard to his adjustment there. I had asked Bob, also, to keep in touch with me, though I was very doubtful that he would do so once he was settled.*

*It is quite possible that Bob will run away once he knows plans are under way for his return to Massachusetts. In this event it would be well for you to report the runaway to the sheriff of San Diego County, and giving his parents name and address and asking they be contacted, when he is picked up. We also should be notified.*

*Don't feel you have "failed" me. Bob demonstrates too uncomfortably that which is so characteristic of these youngsters whose rejection comes early—that is, almost a total inability to really attach positively to adults and other kids. Frequently they start out well, but go off and do just what you are seeing now. I doubt that Bob G's so-called attachment to my Bob would be meaningful in terms of influencing his behavior at those points where he wants his own way, regardless of outcome.*

*Let me know as soon as you have talked with Bob about your correspondence with me about his behavior and plans.*

*(Mrs.) Marabel s. Beck*
*Social Worker*

*Sincerely yours,*
*Marabel S. Beck*

*September 26, 1950*

*Mrs. C. K. Hart*
*Box 286*
*Leucadia, California*

*Dear Alice:*

*Bob seems to be running true to what most foster parents experience in foster home placement—Ups and Downs. Hope things continue as they are. Bob has never been one to study at home.*

*I am enclosing a letter which I recently received from Mr. Garmston. You will note that he asks you to have the work done by a dentist and send the bill to Lytton.*

*Sincerely yours,*
*Lawrence R. Smith, Sr. Captain*
*Superintendent*

*By: (Mrs.) Marabel s. Beck*
*Social Worker*

*Sincerely yours,*
*Marabel S. Beck*
*Social Worker*

*October 5, 1950*

*Mrs. Alice Hart*
*Box 286*
*Leucadia, California*

*Dear Alice:*

*Here is some information to guide you in regard to Bob's planned San Francisco trip. Last Spring I refused him permission to stay overnight with Dino C. because Dino's family lived in one or two rooms with no adequate facilities for housing another person. All the children were at one time removed by Court order from the home, on the basis of general neglect. The neglect consisted mainly of in attendance at school and many health problems. There was never any particular question of the mother's basically good feeling toward the children but she seemed to be totally unable to attend to their little problems and to do what is expected in the way of getting children to school on time and regularly. She is a friendly person but totally unorganized. None of the youngsters were ever in any legal difficulties; there have never been any problems of stealing or running away. Mainly that living conditions were pretty poor and not up to standard. Dino is now at home and as near as I know doing very little. Possibly he is attending continuation school but I don't know for certain. I never felt that Dino and Bob really had anything in common other than the fact that they had both been youngsters living away from home and had the association at Lytton. Dino is a boy of very narrow horizons with few of the capacities that Bob has. In fact Bob once told me that the reason he got interested in Dino was to use him as a tool. I think later the interest changed to one of some feeling for Dino.*

*The other two youngsters he wants to see are probably Gilbert and Shorty. I really question that Bob would get into any particular difficulty on the trip, particularly nothing planned. Anything that might happen comes about accidentally. It does occur to me that probably Bob is going to have to discover for himself and maybe through his visit that he is "growing away" from the old crowd. From your recent letter, I would say that he is developing new interests and that this particular group of boys would have very little in common with those interests that Bob now seems to be showing. None of the other youngsters seem to have any particular ambitions or goals. I would think that if Bob does go it would be much better if he were to arrange to stay at the Y.M.C.A. Hotel in San Francisco. He could make his reservations in advance by mail.*

*I had quite a lengthy letter from Bob's people. Both of them are very anxious that he complete High School and feel that his earnings should be an incidental activity. They suggested that if there were further difficulties in school, that Bob should enlist in the Service when he is of age to do so.*

*Sincerely yours,*
*Lawrence R. Smith, Sr. Captain*
*Superintendent*

*By: (Mrs.) Marabel S. Beck*
*Social Worker*

*Wednesday*
*Nov. 1, 1950*

*Dear Alice:*

*Your letter with the sad news awaited me last night. I had been in S.F.—had made inquiries re: Jim. I hope by now you have insisted on him leaving—frankly I doubt that Jim ever did return to S.F.*

*There are probably agencies in San Diego you could tell Jim to go to— such as Traveler's Air Society, Family Society, etc, but I doubt he would go. If he hasn't left, you may have to call the Sheriff's office and ask for their assistance. I found that Jim is no longer under court custody and if he wanted help in getting straightened out, I am of the opinion that Family and Children's Agency in San Francisco would give counseling services and assist in plans but he must want such help first.*

*My personal self feels like giving him a big kick and my professional self recognizes how mixed up he is. I do know that in common parlance, Jim will sponge. I am embarrassed that he is imposing on you. I found out on return from there that he had been in an auto accident about three weeks ago.*

*Does Bob recognize that it would be unwise for him to get into "league" with Jim? I sure hope he doesn't let his loyalty over ride his good senses.*

*Sincerely,*
*Marabel*

*November 28,*

*Dear Alice,*

*I want to write you fully in regard to Bob but time isn't enough! I have wondered if you want me to write Bob or not. Bob knows why he went to you and not because of the reason he gave. This I could discuss with him and also his relation to home at present. He knows that if he fouls up he is going into the Navy. I think possibly I should write Bob directly about the reality of his situation. And send you a copy so you know how to handle the reactions. What do you think?*

*Marabel*

*Mr. Bob Garmston* *December 5, 1950*

*Box 286 Leucadia, California*

*Dear Bob:*

*. . .No one can be of any assistance to another person in any kind of problem, from as simple a one as staying out late to the extreme one of alcoholism, unless that person wants to utilize the "helper's" services. (Incidentally the same holds true in education— no one can successfully teach a person who doesn't want to learn.) The term "helper" probably isn't a wise selection, for in reality people eventually have to settle their own problems, but each of us, in some fashion or other, utilize others' help in trying to come to a better understanding of ourselves, our relations to other people, and some of the things we do and like. Sometimes other people can help us in trying to understand why we persist in doing things that tend to keep us in trouble. Maybe "help" comes accidentally from just being surrounded by people who are friendly and understanding and to whom you can talk about your worries.*

*Last spring following your trip to San Diego, I deliberately tried to get you to examine some of your trouble spots—mainly the relationship to your parents and experiences, hoping that by hauling these situations out into the open you wouldn't have to continue to fight some of the things and people that eventually can bring you reasonable happiness. I recognized then that you had a lot of questions and uncertainties around your parentage and your adoption. No doubt now you are doing a lot of thinking about "you" and possibly even justifying some of your insistence upon doing what you want to do on the basis that these unpleasant things have happened to you.*

*In the meantime, I think it well for you to remember that personal problems do have to be settled around "fact" of a situation and not always what we wish the situation to be. Maybe you need to look at the facts of your present situation. Right now you are living in a home where the people are interested in you, interested not because of just feeling sorry for you, which is one of the things you mentioned last year as not wanting, but rather because they have liked you. I think the requests they have made of you in terms of hours, compliance with school regulations etc. have not been extreme and are not outside the realm of those required by the majority of parents within a community.*

*Going home is not going to solve the problem of doing what you want when you want for I feel that your parents are going to be more insistent upon compliance with generally accepted rules. Secondly it is well to bear in mind that your placement away from home was the outcome of troubles within the home with your parents. There are many reasons for these problems and I am not placing blame on you nor your parents. The point is, that placement was necessary because of constant friction between the members of the family.*

*I mention this because I think it would be very easy for you to constantly excuse yourself and not realize your own potentialities by feeling that you have been trapped within your own situations.*

*I am witting to your folks today in regard to your coming home.*

*Sincerely Yours,*

*(Mrs.) Marabel S. Beck*

*Social Worker*

*December 5, 1950*

*Mrs. C. K. Hart*
*Box 286*
*Leucadia, California*

*Dear Alice:*

*I am sorry to be so slow in answering your last two letters about Bob. Today I received the third, just as I was preparing to write you. I will write to the Garmstons today and also write to Bob. Enclosed is a copy of the letter to Bob. I think it is very important that Bob write to his people too and try to take some responsibility for his own return home. At this point I would anticipate that the parents will first of all refuse to have Bob return and probably will insist upon him going in the Navy. Their last letter to me, which I sent you a copy of, I believe, conveyed that idea quite definitely. The mother's rejection is deep but has been pretty well covered over by committing most of the responsibility for the whole situation to the father. With the war situation so critical, it may be that Mr. Garmston's position too is uncertain and possibly some move will be in store for them. First of all I do want Bob to write his father regarding his desire to return home. I tried last Spring to encourage Bob to write his father for I thought he should try to get acquainted with him. Possibly the father will respond, but I am not certain.*

*It is very probably that Bob has been staying out because he has been drinking. Just recently I picked up some remarks from one of Kitty's letters to one of the youngsters here, to the effect that Bob had been doing some drinking.*

*Bob always has shut out discussions about his family and walled himself in. Last year after receiving the "bargaining" letter from his mother in which she practically told him he wasn't wanted at home he did open up some. I pointed out that he was probably looking at his father through his mother's eyes and not his. I tried to picture her situation too—that is, the care of a small child with its habits set, etc. at a time when she didn't want this responsibility and consequently the development of a lot of other problems.*

*I am sorry that Bob is being such a source of worry to you. You and King however have been successful with Bob to a degree you do not realize. The fact that Bob even lets you in on his worries about his family is indicative of a lot. I have frequently felt that his extreme insistence upon carrying out his own wishes have been essentially ways of trying to assert his own individuality of which he has many doubts because of the adoption and the circumstantial surroundings of early years. I know the whole matter of who he is and why things have happened to him are certainly uppermost in his mind. I think too that the refusal to really tackle more difficult school subjects has a deeper meaning than just feeling that they are relatively unimportant. You mentioned to me when I was down Bob's fears before giving a talk. I think he shies away from the academic subjects too because he is basically afraid of not succeeding and constantly protects himself against failure by minimizing, being able to say "I could do it if I wanted to but I just don't try." There is probably too an element of trying to establish his own importance by flouting the course of studies, minimizing what others think important.*

*Sincerely yours,*

*Lawrence R. Smith, Sr. Captain*
*Superintendent*

*By: Mrs. Marabel S. Beck*
*Social Worker*

*December 8, 1950*

*431 Dewey St.*
*West Springfield, Mass.*

*Dear Mrs. Beck:*

*Your letter of December 5th received, but none has been received from Bob for the past few months, although letters were written to him and answers requested. Our hope has been that since he has started school there, and as you say is doing well in marks, that he would finish the school year before contemplating any change, whether to come here or join the Navy. We live in a four room house, very small in size and not even the attic is suitable for an extra room as it is unfinished and unheated. There is a possibility that sometime this coming year our landlord may finish the attic, and provide heat facilities there, as we have expressed such a desire. All things point to this possibility not being seriously considered for the winter months, anyway.*

*With this picture of our quarters, we hope you can see that it may be best to postpone sending him home until spring, and preferable after he has finished school.*

*Please let us know if it can be arranged to keep Bob going there until the end of school in spring. In the meantime, we shall do all possible to get that extra room fixed up for use, and furnished suitably, as we do not even have an extra bed or cot at this time.*

*Very truly yours,*
*Lt. and Mrs. J. J. Garmston*

*December 11, 1950*

*Mr. & Mrs. C. K. Hart*

*Box 286*

*Leucadia, California*

*Dear Alice & King:*

*Enclosed are copies of my letter to the Garmstons and a copy of the one I received from them.*

*I received your letter today, and hope the Garmstons cooperate readily, though you note their reluctance to assume responsibility. It is true that Bob at this point tends to utilize the family situation to justify his own actions, and this is the thing I'm concerned about—that he will remain "trapped" in his own rationalizations, even though based on facts.*

*Sincerely yours,*

*(Mrs.) Marabel S. Beck*

*Social Worker*

*December 11, 1950*

*Lt. & Mrs. J. J. Garmston,*
*431 Dewey Street*
*West Springfield, Mass.*

*Dear Lt. and Mrs. Garmston:*

*This morning I received your letter and also one from the Harts. The Harts have definitely requested that Bob leave, preferably the 18$^{th}$ of the month, so there is no alternative, but that Bob go to Massachusetts.*

*I can readily see that your housing must be somewhat uncomfortable, but hope that in this short period intervening, you will be able to work out some sleeping arrangement for Bob.*

*It is imperative that Bob leave Hart's around the 18$^{th}$, so I would suggest that you forward his fare there. Mr. Hart will help Bob with transportation arrangements, if necessary. Mrs. Hart has had a re-occurrence of Rheumatic Fever which complicates the situation.*

*Sincerely yours,*
*Lawrence R. Smith, Sr. Captain*
*Superintendent*

*By:* *Mrs. Marabel S. Beck*

*Social Worker*

❈ ❈ ❈

*December 11, 1950*

*Mr. Robert Garmston*
*Box 286,*
*Leucadia California.*

*Dear Bob:*

*Today I received a letter from your folks requesting your return. Their housing situation is crowded, but I'm requesting today that they forward you money for your trip home.*

*Apparently you have never sent your clothing sizes home, for your parents asked for sizes and I really don't know.*

*Let me know what arrangements you make for returning. I have not gone into detail regarding reasons for requesting your return; I did mention your desire to see them and the difficulty around time limits.*

*Sincerely yours,*
*LAWRENCE R. SMITH, Sr. Captain*
*Superintendent*

*By: (Mrs.) Marabel S. Beck*
*Social Worker*

*January 9, 1951*

*Mr. & Mrs. C. K. Hart*
*Box 286*
*Leucadia, California*

*Dear Alice and King:*

*Yesterday morning I discovered to my unhappiness and certainly yours that our bookkeeper did not send the December board check for Bob. I am very sorry, for I know how important it is to be able to plan on having money at a needed time in which funds are low. By this time, I hope you have received the check. I purposely had it cover Bob's period of absence too and believe this justifiable in terms of the extras you have provided and the essentials that the $45.00 does not cover.*

*The arrival of your letter on January 5 seemed to crystallize Bob's desire to return to Leucadia. He had been planning to do so, though I thought he still had many conflicts around giving up the idea of wanting to go back to Massachusetts even though it meant sending himself. I myself have had my doubts that it was really fair in terms of your total situation for Bob to return, somehow or other the letter tended to make him feel that he should be part of some of your troubles too. He expressed himself as wanting to get a job, after school and on Saturdays if possible, so that he would be able to cake care of more of his own needs and possibly be of a little help otherwise.*

*At first Bob thought only of going to Massachusetts. Although we would have been in a position to only send him one way, though this too would have incurred the possibility of legal liability in event of an accident in route, Bob did not feel he wanted to take the chance of being "stuck" on the East Coast but would want to return out here. He has very strong feeling in needing to determine for himself what his parents' feelings actually are for him, though I felt that at the same time it was almost a little more than he could really take. Seeing the actual wire probably made him realize the validity of any feelings that he may have had in the past that they really are not interested in him.*

*He tends to express however that he has always felt, up until recently, that he was wanted there. He has accepted at face value any reasons given to him for placement away from home. In view of the total situation, I think he functions amazingly well and from experience with a large number of severely rejected children, Bob apart from his need to be resistant to direction, he is better adjusted than most. I was reluctant to send a youngster back to such severely rejecting parents, even though they are legally responsible.*

*We talked considerably about the points of difference between you and Bob. Bob does seem to understand your viewpoint and said he had decided before coming North that drinking and late hours were to be things of the past. He seems to have made some identification with your family and standards and I think that this was a factor in him wanting to share some of the current difficulties. I hope however he does not increase your worries. He is a little concerned and ashamed, I think, that he didn't work too hard at school this past term and feels that he will disappoint you in his performance.*

*Today I wrote his father in regard to the father's legal obligations, requested an increase to $50.00 for board, money for an allowance for Bob and also money for clothing for Bob. I have made reference to his Naval obligations, feel that he may respond. In the meantime too, I intend to write San Diego Agencies regarding referral of Bob for planning* *and counseling in event you return to Michigan or find it not feasible to have him. I think Bob is facing pretty straight the fact that the parents are trying to drop out of the picture and that he is probably going to have to be on his own. Of course under California law, the father is responsible for support until the boy is twenty-one years of age.*

*It was unfortunate that Jim has done what he has. I am not surprised however but only wish you had not been his victim. I am glad you wrote me, for it does give me some opportunity to bring up what I thought might be happening in relation to Bob too. I feel that in some ways Jim tried to undermine Bob's position with you, by trying to point out Bob's past inadequacies while at the same time Jim remained the "good boy." Of the two boys, it has been our experience that Bob is basically more honest and generally stable. Jim has been an "extremist," is able to verbalize a much better adjustment and understanding of situations than his performance indicates. He has never met any of his small financial commitments, though there have been many promises and on occasions reminders. He owes me money personally from other situations and also owes small amounts to Lytton for special medical needs that were done in connection with him entering the Service.*

*I have suggested that he try to discuss with you voluntarily those matters over which you seem to disagree. He is currently open to discussion than he was at the time he went to your home. Has respect for your opinions even though he may not always conform readily. Bob is essentially a nonconformist, I think, though some of his nonconformity is pretty normal adolescent behavior. I hope you will understand that we don't hold you responsible nor could his parents actually for any particular difficulties or accidents that might occur to Bob while living in your home. I can understand however that if he incurs displeasure in the community that it does reverberate on you and your family and this I think should definitely be discussed. I think too that Bob could assume more responsibility for helping you around the house than he has. Possibly it will be necessary to give him some definite responsibilities. I talked briefly with him about this and I think at this point he needs the discipline of a definite assignment for he does not particularly see things that need to be done nor feel the urge to go ahead, only spasmodically. At the same time he does recognize and can verbalize the fact that he doesn't take as much responsibility as he should nor be as thoughtful of other people as he would really like to be. Some of this comes from many years of institutional living in which it is almost necessary to do so many things for the children.*

*Sincerely yours,*
*LAWRENCE R. SMITH, Sr. Captain*

*Superintendent*

*By: (Mrs.) Marabel S. Beck*
*Social Worker*

*January 18, 1951*

*Mr. & Mrs. C. K. Hart*
*P.O. Box 286*
*Leucadia, CA*

*Dear Alice & King:*

*Bob will probably tell you about the next chapter in the Garmston saga: Briefly, the father is forwarding money for fare to Massachusetts the last of this month, wants Bob ready to return around the 2nd or 3rd of February. This is the outcome of asking for more support and pointing out legal responsibilities.*

*This must be terribly confusing for Bob and he will need your help in meeting the situation, I think. I will find out what sources are available for Bob in Springfield if the situation is intolerable.*

*Do you think it might be well for you to let the school principal or counselor know why Bob is again leaving school?*

*Sincerely,*

*Lawrence R. Smith, Sr. Captain*

*Superintendent*

*By: (Mrs.) Marabel S. Beck*

*Social Worker.*

*2-1-51*

*Dear Alice:*

*[As you know, Mr. Garmston phoned last evening, requesting in a most arrogant Napoleonic manner that Bob return East directly from Leucadia. I asked Bob to return the ticket I sent him to come up to Lytton. The father is angry with us, I think, and probably wants to prevent any contact.*

*Bob is probably going to be in for considerable difficulty in unhappy experiences. How do you think he will react to such? I don't want to encourage his delinquency—but do want him to know that if the going is too tough—we could use a milker! Could you convey the idea with subtlety?*

*Marabel*

*2-15-51*

*Dear Alice, Sure hope things work out. You should see our file. Mrs. G.'s expression of hatred for Mr. G. and Bob, and Mr. G.'s similar expressions for Mrs. G.*

*I'm sure your letter helped. Any positive statements we made about Lytton were always resisted.*

*Marabel*

March 14: *Hand written note to the Harts from Marabel. Bob is enlisting in Navy. Didn't last long in Massachusetts.*

*Wednesday 3-14*

*Dear Harts:*

*You have probably heard that Bob is enlisting in the Navy. Bob B had a request for a reference— and I had a short note from Bob to the effect that he had applied for enlistment and was working, pending decision. Didn't take long!*

*How are you guys? Is Larry better?*

*Had a bull calf yesterday. Am sending you some meat—will probably leave next Monday.*

*Marabel*

*(Endnotes)*

1 Garmston, Lynne. (July 2009) Personal correspondence.